PARTY WEIRD

FESTIVALS & FRINGE GATHERINGS

OF AUSTIN

Howie Richey

HOWIE RICHEY 10-31-14

THE
History
PRESS

Published by The History Press
Charleston, SC 29403
www.historypress.net

Back cover, bottom right: The Armadillo World Headquarters opened in South Austin in August
1970. *Courtesy Jim Franklin.*

First published 2014

Manufactured in the United States

ISBN 978.1.62619.652.0

Library of Congress CIP data applied for.

This verbal Valentine goes out to the city I adore and to all celebrants therein who persist in carrying the torch. Viva Austin!

For Lina, my lovely.

Contents

FOREWORD

Austin was born to be a party town.

In 1842, some six years after the Battle of the Alamo, a tug of war arose about where the new capital should be located. As the Mexican army continued to invade the sovereign republic, a worried President Sam Houston called a special session of the Texas Congress. It was time to move the Texas Archives to a safer place, he told them. To Houston, natch.

The feisty citizens of Austin objected and formed a committee of safety, warning government heads they weren't to be fooled with. Sure enough, in early December of that year, twenty-two Texas Rangers rode into Austin after dark and loaded three wagons with the precious archives. They nearly got away with it, save for a sharp-eyed boardinghouse owner named Angelina Eberley. She spotted the furtive movement and jumped into immediate action.

Eberley loaded the six-pounder cannon that stood at what is now Sixth Street and Congress Avenue and fired it, attempting to stop the theft and rally the committee. She didn't aim well and blew a hole in the side of the General Land Office, but the ruckus woke the town. A vigilante group quickly assembled and chased the rangers north to Williamson County, where they were cornered near Brushy Creek and ultimately surrendered the archives.

That New Year's Eve, Austin threw a party that both celebrated the town's victory and affirmed the citizenry's commitment to its identity. The scant details available suggest dancing, revelry and a fiddler or two on hand—all the ingredients for a good time around a good cause.

And if you asked Bill Narum, he'd tell you Austin was weird from the very start, too. The late artist, best known for his ZZ Top album covers, often opined that the earliest businesses in Austin were a music hall and a printing press. The press founders quarreled and one left, opening a competing press. Therefore, Narum reasoned, the first dynamic in Austin was music and alternative press. How weird is that?

Even by the late 1800s, when Austin settled into a semblance of its present persona, an area of downtown at the river and just west of Congress Avenue known as "Mexico," or more commonly "Guy Town," emerged. Guy Town sported pleasure houses of all ethnicities plus saloons where player pianos or Victrolas played—a seedier, more sinful precursor to today's Sixth Street entertainment district.

In other words, to party in Austin has deep historical significance—OK, perhaps not that deep, but notable nonetheless. It didn't hurt that the University of Texas annually attracted thousands of students eager to celebrate or that the capitol drew party-hearty politicos from all corners of the state into the city's limits. By the time the music scene for which the town is so famous came into being, it was merely a soundtrack for the party that had been happening since the city's birth.

Party Weird shapes into cogent reading the various celebrations that make Austin unique. This is a town where Eeyore the donkey of Winnie-the-Pooh fame has been fêted every April since 1964. Football at the University of Texas brings its barbecue bacchanals in the autumn. It's home to spring break for the music industry—South by Southwest, currently the most popular festival in the world—and the attendant fall music festival, Austin City Limits.

How do I know? For most of the years between 1983 and 2014, I directed the biggest musicians' party around during South by Southwest—the *Austin Chronicle*'s Austin Music Awards show. During those years, Austin ballooned from being a musical anomaly in Texas to a force that affected the entire music industry. That's where I learned one measure of a party's success is who's on the guest list: 2014's SXSW featured Lady Gaga and Kanye West.

Nowadays, Austin feels like a party in the making, 24/7. When one event is winding down, another is gearing up, creating a nonstop cycle of activities year round. And it's not simply festivals, fairs, Formula One and football games—the sheer number of benefits and fundraisers in this town featuring named performers offers 'round-the-calendar fun, too.

If Austin needed one more way to distinguish itself, it does so as Texas's premier party town with the violet crown. So bring along a couple of friends and join in. After all, two's company, but three's a party.

—Margaret Moser, *Austin Chronicle*

PREFACE

The idea of writing a history of celebrations began when I was old enough to appreciate what a party is and why it was different from everyday life. Growing up in a typical suburban South Texas family exposed me to the usual kiddie birthday parties and small-scale events in school. Mom and Dad were fairly social and would go out to office parties or the like, but their peers' use of alcohol and tobacco—which bothered my parents—raised barriers about what was acceptable in our home. I can remember only a few times when other folks came over, mainly for dinner. More often, however, my father invited in several of his fellow audiophiles to "spin a few" records, especially after some innovation of Dad's sophisticated sound system.

My most vivid example of the frolic possible in a social gathering came from Rowan and Martin's *Laugh-In*, a hilarious 1960s ensemble comedy show that broke numerous social barriers in its time. Every episode featured a party scene in which dancing and music and interaction ensued, all suddenly stopping any time some reveler would deliver a one liner. Ah, so that's what a party is all about, I mused.

Secondary school gave me glimpses into different ways of celebration, mainly with fellow students and in church. Adult-sponsored dances were of paramount importance, but I also loved simply hanging out at the liberal Darden home, just chatting with my fellow speech club chums.

When I got to Austin in September 1971, fresh out of high school, I discovered the wild side of university dormitories and living away from parental oversight. There was no shortage of social occasions open to my buddies and me. With so many mixers, football games and joyrides to choose from, I gradually learned which of them were worth attending and which to avoid. In either case, I was imprinted with Austin's champion party-city status, a reputation that continues today.

Fast-forward to my days of apartment dwelling and a growing desire to become not just a party attendee but a host as well—and not just a regular host but a super one; not just of any regular old party but of elaborate ones. Truth be told, I made some errors in the beginning, wrongly thinking that a few colored lights and several good LPs on the stereo would a good party make. But I learned from those mistakes, and you'll find out later in this tome what happened.

Skip a bunch more frames to the fall of 2013, when Christen Thompson of The History Press contacted me about writing a book about one of my tours. We volleyed several ideas, but it seemed to me that thousands of pages are already written about Texas travel. I saw no reason to be just another swimmer in those crowded waters. It then occurred to me to explore that other passion of mine, the art and science of festivity. To my knowledge, no one has ever attempted a history of Austin celebrations.

So here it is. Not comprehensive by any means, the tales told here represent but a small slice of the huge number of get-togethers this creative city has spawned since my arrival in 1971. With luck, if the story appeals to enough readers, more of this subject's history will emerge.

Meanwhile, let the party continue.

ACKNOWLEDGEMENTS

Hooray for those who helped and inspired: Myra McIlvain and Dan and Rennie Quinn served as readers and commentators, saving me much embarrassment. Thanks to all the folks and friends I interviewed, including Leeann Atherton, Fletcher Clark, Jim Franklin, the Snuffs, Joe Bryson, Kerry Awn, Grace Park, Jim O'Brien, Nancy Higgins, Cody Johnson and Michael McGeary. I appreciate the treasure-trove of repositories available here, such as the Austin History Center, Texas State Library and Archives, South Austin Popular Culture Center (Leea and Henry) and the Center for American History (John Wheat). The staff patiently answered my same questions over and over. Big hugs also go to Margaret Moser, Joe Nick Patoski, Eddie Wilson and the amazing poster artists and musicians who contributed to this project. Additionally, I'm obliged to my family, friends and co-workers for their encouragement and patience. I think it's time for a celebration!

INTRODUCTION

For anyone driving north on Interstate 35 from points south, one of the best introductory views of the city of Austin happens at the curve under the Riverside Drive overpass. There, for a brief few thousand feet, the highway runs north and slightly west before another curve shifts the road northeast again. Like going through a magic gateway, you see this City of Dreams stretching before you as you cross the Colorado River. In 1971, the town was home to some 263,000 souls. In those days, the round tower of the Holiday Inn on your left might have struck you as a bit unusual. Any such inkling of novelty, however, would only grow as the city's spirit captivated you.

If you came into town on this same route once a decade, you'd see dramatic differences in the skyline. Those changes would seem to accelerate after 2001 and proceed exponentially by 2011 and into 2014. Whereas the capitol building and the University of Texas tower were the dominant structures for more than forty years, now other edifices reign supreme. Joseph Campbell remarked that the tallest buildings in a city indicated the most important concerns to that populace.[1] In the Middle Ages, the church stood the highest; during the eighteenth century Enlightenment, tallest was the government center. In the late 1900s, banks dominated. In Austin today, condos peer down on everything else.

All these signs point to tremendous growth in the Austin metropolitan area. Like other midsized cities in America experiencing rapid expansion, this place is grappling with the loss of former stability and innocence, in a sense. Longtime residents worry about the city losing its soul and character. What's special and unique about this city, and how can Austin's very essence remain intact? *In how we play* comes a partial answer.

This book aims to give background and meaning to known and unknown activities in one of the world's best cities for entertaining. Austin, Texas, is renowned for many things, such as live music, a strong economy, amazing art, unique heritage, outstanding educational facilities and beautiful environs. It also is home to world-class events like Formula One, South by Southwest (SXSW) and Austin City Limits. Similarly well known beyond its borders is Austin's vibrant underground social scene, which expresses itself in frequent soirées both public and private, monthly and annual. This book catalogues those obscure, outlandish happenings with interviews, photos and specific traditions of each affair. The focus is on the countercultural strata that inform Austin's progressive weirdness. I will more explicitly attempt to define *party* and show its relation to a festival or concert. As well, there will be a section on extinct sprees. For broader context, you will learn how this town's celebratory spirit evolved.

Here's the specific meaning of *party* as used in this book. For our purposes, parties possess all or most of these elements:

⇨ An invitation, which could include art, a poster or an ad
⇨ A guest or mailing list
⇨ A reason, occasion or theme with related ambiance
⇨ Costumes, decorations, colors
⇨ A place or venue, recurring or mobile
⇨ Food, drink, other
⇨ An activity or entertainment
⇨ Music, dancing
⇨ A progression or schedule[2]

The word *party* comes from *part*. By definition, a party is a specific set of people, not just everyone or anyone. That segment of folks is usually invited—not compelled—to attend. A party is a social time, not one to work or accomplish anything, per se, although being sociable can convey benefits after the party's over. A *festival* is like a party, only bigger and longer lasting. I like to think of a festival as a series of related, small key groups nested inside a larger event.

Let me tell you just how amazing our parties are. To do that, I'll tell you how amazing this city is, identify the types of people it attracts and then show how amazing gatherings can't help but develop here. To assist our thinking, here's a ready word to learn and use: *topophilia*. It means a strong sense of place, which often becomes mixed with an impression of cultural identity among certain peoples and a love of certain aspects of such a place.[3] Austinites possess this awareness in spades. We trumpet social innovation. Here, we celebrate ourselves, one another and this locale. In Austin, you need a separate calendar just for social activities

But what do you mean by *weird*?

To fully grok Austin's unique strangeness, it's best to start this story with some pure history. As every Texas schoolchild knows,[4] the Lone Star flag flew over a sovereign republic for nearly a decade, from 1836 to 1845. The republic's capital moved several times during the first few years of independence but seemed fairly settled in "Houston City" during the term of the first president, Sam Houston. However, by Texas law, Houston the man could not succeed himself. It was the idea of Texas's second president, Mirabeau B. Lamar, to move the seat of government to a place closer to the new nation's center. As vice president in 1838, Lamar had visited the then-tiny village (in truth, merely several log cabins) of Waterloo to hunt buffalo. Like so many who were to come, Lamar totally fell in love with the surroundings: hills to the west, a fine river running through, timber, fresh springs and abundant wildlife. Under Lamar's influence, the Texas Congress voted to found a new capital city named for Stephen F. Austin, the Anglo "Father of Texas" who had pioneered American immigration to the area during Mexican rule in the 1820s. Austin the city is special not only because

Austin's ever-changing skyline appeared this way in May 2014. *Author's collection.*

it's one of only three towns in the world built to be the capital of a republic {Name the other two.[5]}, but also because its location was chosen on pure aesthetics more than practicality.[6]

Carving a new capital at what many considered the edge of the known universe began in early February 1839. By October 17 of that year, enough crude structures were in place along freshly cleared dirt pathways to welcome the Texas government. A long parade of wagons full of elected officials, staff, furniture and boxes full of papers snaked its way into the baby city from points east on the newly christened Pecan Street and stopped at Congress Avenue. There, at Bullock's "hotel," itself a cluster of rustic log buildings, the guests and original citizens held a triumphant dinner. No fewer than thirty-nine toasts were raised to the new capital.

We've been raising our glasses to this place ever since. The town began with a party, and it never ended.

Now dig this: Items enclosed in {braces} are trivia questions answered in the Notes.

A Note on Substances

When ingested, certain chemicals tend to alter human perception and behavior. Social situations often include social lubricants. Caffeine, for instance, enhances sharp thinking and conversation. Alcohol, for another, relaxes the muscles and suppresses inhibitions. Though by definition both are "drugs," they're legal and generally civilly acceptable. A third substance, cannabis, is ubiquitously available and its use widely observed, but it is illegal almost everywhere. While official strictures are slowly changing worldwide, reefer is still against the law in Texas. However, certain parts of the state interpret the statutes somewhat more liberally. Austin and Houston are places where a police officer holds the option of issuing a citation to, but not arresting, someone found in possession of two ounces or fewer of pot.[7]

It would be completely inaccurate for any publication to deny that the inhalation of smoldering ganja happens at parties or festivals in a happy city such as Austin. It would be just as wrong to believe that the herb hasn't made a difference in the creative energy here, opening modes of thinking and imaginations to heights not previously possible. Austin's freewheeling, rebellious reputation insists that the "Willie Nelson, laid-back atmosphere" is the rule here rather than the exception. The joke used to be that there was a two-joint minimum just to get inside the city limits. With inflation these days, it's probably three.

This disclaimer means to acknowledge the prevalence of Mary Jane, to recognize its influence but to neither encourage nor defend its acquaintance. Now that we're straight on that, we can move on.

PART I

DEFUNCT FUNCTIONS

1

1890s

Here we look into the past at events that helped cement Austin's reputation as a partying mecca.

Before modern people invented the term "party animal," Austin had its share of active celebrants. Throughout the city's existence, newcomers and residents found plenty of social activities in which to mingle and participate. Around town were several beer gardens, most founded by Germans and other Europeans: Scholz, Pressler's, Turner, Jacoby's and Buass. These were family-centered establishments that often brewed their own beer and provided musical entertainment. Hyde Park, one of the city's first official suburbs, featured a small lake for pleasure boating, a bandstand for concerts and a racetrack for wagering. {Which Austin street recalls that last place?[8]}

Let's go way back to a time out of mind. In the last decade of the nineteenth century, two individuals called Austin home and contributed to the festive atmosphere in artistic ways. They were William Sidney Porter and Elisabet Ney. The former gets but a brief summary shortly and a big spread later, but the woman deserves great accolades now.

One of the city's first prominent residents to live in an unconventional manner was Elisabet Ney, a beautiful and charming woman of Westphalian birth who was a prominent female sculptor in her German homeland during a time when few women were able to devote their lives to art. With sheer talent and innate curiosity, she achieved unusual success creating stone statues of European philosophers, musicians, literati and royalty. Married to Scots physician and scientist Edmund Montgomery in 1863, she and her life partner investigated down-to-earth living and romantic ideals. For Edmund's health, the pair moved to the United States in 1871, living first in Georgia in a kind of commune.

When the Peach State didn't satisfy their deep naturalistic longings, they searched other places in the country and discovered a dilapidated southern plantation house called Liendo[9] near Hempstead, Texas. This they purchased in 1873, and for the next twenty years, they farmed and raised their one surviving son, Lorne, with Ney setting aside her art. Alas, the bucolic operation barely broke even, and the boy later became estranged.

At the invitation of former Texas governor Oran M. Roberts, Ney in 1893 visited Austin and felt the city's allure. She missed her art and realized that she could resume her career in this already creative environment. Purchasing two and a half acres at the edge of the new Hyde Park subdivision north of downtown, she designed and built a studio home that resembles both a Greek temple and a European castle. She christened it Formosa from an earlier time she spent in Portugal. After a commission from the State of Texas to execute in marble the likenesses of Stephen F. Austin and Sam Houston, she was able to work profusely, eventually producing scores of renowned pieces.

Today, the Austin and Houston statues welcome visitors from the state capitol's South Foyer to the Rotunda. The men and the works represented Ney's return to the world of art, as well as the beginnings of true fine art in the Lone Star State. She came out of self-imposed exile and isolation into the larger world and into the young city's growing sphere of influence.

Besides her precise art, Ney was known for her unusual lifestyle. If you admired her, her novel ways pleased you. If you were a regular guy, however, you'd have been appalled. Even though she was Dr. Montgomery's civil wife, she always insisted on being called "Miss Ney." She wore velvet hats and flowing robes, short (just below the knee) black tunics or pants with knee-high boots. A minimalist, she ate simple meals of clabber and juice. Since she came from Germany, Ney found Texas damn hot, so she'd either sleep on a cot on the roof, a hammock in the tower or out back in a wooden-floored tent. Anytime she rode a horse, which was fairly frequently, it was bareback and astride, not sidesaddle.

For the purposes of this book's theme, you can place yourself inside one of Elisabet's social activities. From the Ney Museum website:

> *Many friends were drawn to the delightful and interesting "Miss Ney."*
> *Ney's Formosa soon became the site of creative impulses of a different,*

Elisabet Ney at work in her studio with a plaster study of Stephen F. Austin behind her. From a painting inside the Texas capitol. *Author's collection.*

but no less important, nature: those that arise out of the meetings of minds and shared aspirations. Those meetings have been described by Bride Neill Taylor:

"In the little drawing room of the studio a sort of salon established itself, where visitors were sure to meet the most cultivated, the most interesting, the

most distinguished men and women of whom the little capital city could boast…The little salon in Hyde Park became the natural gathering place of such men and women as were capable of foreseeing a new Texas."

Of their banter, Taylor writes:

"The conversation played back and forth between the artist and her guests on the subjects dealing mostly with the larger aspects of life, which gave to many a listener a broadening of intellectual vision, a human livening up of already acquired knowledge, which otherwise had lain dormant within as dead and dried up book-lore."

It is not surprising, and quite interesting, to find Elisabet Ney's studio described as a "salon" in 1892 Austin, where "saloon" was one of Austin's most widely known attributes. And yet, Taylor's account of the meetings at Formosa very aptly describes the salons of Elisabet Ney's earlier life in Berlin and Munich. One might say that Elisabet Ney, among her many contributions, introduced the first European salon to Austin in 1892.[10]

That, and she was also famed for her parties. In typical Teutonic fashion, Ney labored hard and without distraction when she worked but played merrily in her off hours. Friends who stopped by enjoyed floating in boats on

Miss Ney loved entertaining Austinites of any age. *Courtesy Elisabet Ney Museum.*

Elisabet Ney (right) chats with friends over tea. *Courtesy Elisabet Ney Museum.*

the little lake she'd created with a dam across Waller Creek. If you had been there, you'd have experienced stimulating conversation about politics and art in the company of professors, socialites and civic leaders. Doubtless you would have marveled at the rustic picnic tables that held her contrastingly fine china. You would have enjoyed the music from the orchestra playing above in the tower.[11]

If you asked her opinion on domestic duties, she would answer, "Women are fools…to be bothered with housework. Look at me. I sleep in a hammock which requires no making up. I break an egg and sip it raw. I make lemonade in a glass and then rinse it, and my housework is done for the day."

Meanwhile, downtown, William Sydney Porter, the writer who became famous as O. Henry, lived in Austin from 1884 until 1897. Born in North Carolina in 1862, Porter came to Texas to improve his health. While working as a cowboy in the South Texas county of La Salle, he carried a dictionary everywhere he went and spent much time in his employer's private library. When Porter got to the Capital City, he toiled at a series of nonliterary odd jobs but published a humor weekly called the *Rolling Stone*. Paving the way for partygoers to come, Will was quite the active man about town, taking part in that era's diverse social activities. He was often seen relaxing with a beverage in one of the city's pleasant beer gardens or singing bass in church choirs and with three other men in the Hill City Quartet. That vocal group would often serenade young ladies, one of whom, Athol Estes, Will married in 1885.

William Sydney Porter gained fame as the short story writer O. Henry. *Public domain.*

The couple and their daughter, Margaret, rented a simplified Eastlake cottage on Cedar Street for several years before time and circumstance rent the family asunder. While working as a teller in a local bank, Porter was tried and convicted of embezzlement, for which he spent time in an Ohio penitentiary. It was there that he adopted his pen name. Porter never returned to Austin after 1898, but several locales hereabouts, such as the Old Land Office, became immortalized in his surprise-ending short stories.[12]

We don't know if Mr. Porter ever met Miss Ney, but since the city contained barely twenty-three thousand inhabitants, they might have at least heard of each other. She had her salon,[13] but Will hung out in a saloon—the Bismarck on Congress Avenue.

2
Aqua Fest

Almost every city throws an annual party to showcase all that makes the place special. Typical of these celebrations are parades, carnivals, fireworks displays, beauty pageants and history reenactments—all backed by the local chamber of commerce or similar civic organization. In Corpus Christi, for instance, the big yearly event is Buccaneer Days, which ties together the town's coastal habitat and the heritage of pirates, sailing, beachcombing and fishing. San Antonio hosts Fiesta, a nod to Hispanic and Germanic influences, agriculture and Texas independence. From 1962 until 1998, Austin presented the Aqua Festival.

Still a city of merely 200,000 people in the early '60s, Austin was proud of its water resources. With the completion of the Longhorn Dam in 1961, seven bodies of beautiful, clear Colorado River water {What are they?[14]} offered local and visiting folks fun in the sun. Aqua Fest took place in early August, the hottest month of the Texas year and a good time to seek the coolness that water provided. In addition to the above-mentioned standard fare, Aqua Fest also offered a plethora of amphibious activities, including water skiing expos, speedboat races and a river parade.

Over the years, the festival changed emphasis and expanded its programs. If you were living in Austin in those days, you probably remember the motorcycle races, pet parade, Sailing Club Regatta and golf tournament. One of your fondest recollections was buying your Skipper Pin, a two-inch plastic boat steering wheel attached to a roped anchor, rendered in a different color combination every year. This

The Austin Aqua Festival held two parades: one on land, such as this one from the 1960s, and another afloat. *Courtesy LCRA.*

insignia gave you discounts on tickets and concessions and became a collector's item over time.

Controversy brewed, however, over the drag boat races, which happened on Town Lake (now called Lady Bird Lake) east of the Interregional (IH-35). In those years before gentrification, the East Side was home to much of the city's black and Hispanic populations, who were by and large not well represented politically. With crowds approaching the tens of thousands and with increased traffic and concerns about noise, East Siders protested. When city fathers paid little heed, demonstrations erupted into violence. The speedboats had left town for good by 1979.

Probably the best recalled of Aqua Fest happenings were the theme nights. Each evening's entertainment centered on a specific central Texas ethnic or interest group. Thus came evenings of Czech, Western, German, Latino, black heritage and even Italian emphasis, though that last one was a bit of a stretch. Willie Nelson played Western Night in 1973. By the early '80s, the center of activity had moved to what's now called Auditorium Shores, where another set of neighbors begrudgingly put up with increased traffic, congestion and racket. Multiple stages with multiple bands prefigured a future Austin event that we'll get to soon enough.

Ethnic nights devolved into big-name mega-concerts in the late '80s. Crowds reached a maximum of more than 250,000. In the early '90s, with civic sponsorship withdrawn, ticket prices went up, and attendance came down. After struggling with relevance and mismanagement, Aqua Fest went the way of the dodo in 1998.[15]

3
Aralyn Hughes

Sometimes, parties center on one particular host or personality. Aralyn Hughes is a thespian, visual artist, dancer, writer and realtor. She got involved with the city's theater community in 1976, the year she arrived from Oklahoma. She became famous around town because of her unusual antics, uninhibited attire, intensely decorated dwellings, pig-themed art car, pet pig and comedic autobiographical shows. For her ongoing expressions of individuality and creativeness, Aralyn is called Austin's "Queen of Weird."

If you were to ask her what her parties were all about, she'd hearken back to the 1980s with a quote found on the bathroom wall at Liberty Lunch, a now-razed Austin nightclub: "Cocaine is God's way of telling you you're making too much money."

She began with Gemini parties in the early '80s for five or six women, herself included, who were born under that duplicitous sign. These events moved to and from different places. She then conspired with ten other people to throw Halloween parties, which were supremely popular but strictly private.

"The invitations were so coveted that people who didn't get one were willing to pay to get one because, in order to get into the party, you needed two things: an invitation and a costume," Aralyn says. "There was a high demand to get access to those invitations."

Anyone showing up without both a ticket and a costume was denied entry. This ensured exclusivity and control. Sometimes four hundred invitations went out, so Ms. Hughes would rent an entire nightclub or assembly building, such as Antone's, Zilker Clubhouse, Louie's on the Lake, Carpenter Hall or Whiskey River. Once underway, entertainment such as her tap dance troupe would perform, a live band would play (for free, because they were her friends), a cash bar would open and people who brought their own stimulants would consume them. She never furnished drugs, but lots were there.

One year, Aralyn and her pet pig, Ara (which she named after her mother), went to a Halloween party as Pork and Beans. The pig wanted to be the beans and Aralyn to be the pork, but Aralyn wouldn't do it. "I absolutely put

Aralyn Hughes entertains friends and admirers in her apartment every year on her birthday. *Author's collection.*

my foot down. I'm not gonna be the pig. You have to be the pig."

"I live my life as a canvas," she explains. "I paint on it as I go, whether it's visual art, stage performance, film or writing. I'm guided by a sense of adventure and curiosity, and being in my sixties has done nothing to change that."[16]

More recently, Aralyn lived in the heart of the central city on Congress Avenue a couple blocks south of the capitol grounds. In the historic Larmour Block {Who was Larmour?[17]} between Ninth and Tenth Streets stands a row of 1870s carved-limestone storefronts with apartments upstairs. Her home was a veritable museum to herself, packed with memorabilia from every part of her past life, including a childhood tricycle. In the front facing the street was the real estate office with its computer, desk and cabinets full of files. In the middle was the boudoir of colorful dresses and accessories, including dozens of pairs of shoes. The kitchen occupied the back, where a door led to the parking area behind the building. To this loft, Aralyn invited people over for talk and drinks, and here she participated in another annual event.

A much-anticipated celebration is the yearly Holiday Sing-Along and Downtown Stroll, which occurs typically on December's first Saturday. Sponsored by radio station KUT/KUTX, the local National Public Radio affiliate, the night commences with veteran broadcaster John Aielli's leading carols and other seasonal favorites from the capitol building's south steps. That's followed by the official illumination of the evergreen tree with a light show at Eleventh Street. Then the crowd migrates toward the Colorado River along what we Austinites call the Main Street of Texas. Most of the shops stay open until late, and street musicians, dancers and marching bands provided tunes, moves and cadence. If you knew Aralyn when she lived above Congress, you could step up the stairs next to the art gallery and visit as she held court in her celebrity-filled space.

These days, Aralyn retains her real estate practice and performs in one-woman shows, storytelling engagements and films. In mid-2014, she published a book, *Kid Me Not*, about women who came of age in the 1960s but chose to remain childfree.[18] Her parties and swinging times continue.

4
CORN FEST

O n the west end of West Sixth Street between West Lynn and MoPac Boulevard stood a couple of big old houses, in which, in the early 1970s, there lived a creative bunch of young people.

We were Team Bean Palace, composed of Raymond "T.R." Tatum, his lovely sister Debo (a damn fine baker), and me. For you youngsters and transplants out there who might be wondering what the Bean Palace might have been, let me say that it comprised the eastern—and much saner—half of Succotash Central. It was the bungalow on West Sixth that was decorated with the cumulus clouds against azure sky, with the floating pinto bean and crawdad [riding it] above the porch. Our neighbors to the west were the Corn Palace, inhabited by Art (last name Eddy), Artly (as in Snuff), and Artist (Tommy B). Their domicile was an artistic homage to maize and site of the largest collection of corn memorabilia in the free world. The Shiner delivery guys would make a once-weekly stop to replenish the beer supply, and it also held the world's only Lid-O-Matic[19] dispenser. Together, as Succotash Central, we put on some of the most outrageous parties and marathon Risk tournaments this burg has witnessed, rivaled only by Cliff and Ellen (Turner) Scott's famous insect and clown costume theme parties across the street. For those location freaks in the crowd, the whole block is now a barren wasteland inhabited by the Heartless Bank, just before MoPac.[20]

Official event T-shirts were signed and numbered by the artist. *Courtesy Tommy Bauman.*

The first Corn Festival honored the one-year anniversary of Richard Nixon's resignation. It was on Saturday, August 9, 1975, in the backyard of the Corn Palace, at 1721 West Sixth. The in-house sketcher, Tommy B., drew illustrations for posters and T-shirts, the sale of which financed beer purchases. In the usual Austin arrangement, folks brought potluck food, and the bands played for free to get noticed.

After five years at the original site, the party moved a couple times but enjoyed great success for another half decade on Del Curto Street, an undulating lane through a hilly section of town off South Lamar. It was a pie-shaped lot, seventy feet narrow at the curb but seven hundred feet wide toward the back with plenty of space. Every year, the T-shirt was created

Attendees were never disappointed by those corny happenings. *Courtesy Tommy Bauman.*

by a different artist. That list of talent sounds like a who's who of Austin posterists: Danny Garrett, Micael Priest, Rick Turner, Guy Juke and Kerry Awn, to name a few. The screen-printed designs featured a "secret color," which was glow-in-the-dark paint.

If you had been enjoying chips, salsa and beer late one afternoon in the spring of 2014 at Maria's Taco Xpress, you might have eavesdropped on a conversation between Artly Snuff; his wife, Theresa; and Kerry Awn:

> *Artly: The biggest Corn Fests were down on Del Curto, like in the '80s. We figured it wasn't a success unless either the police broke up the party or we found someone lying in the bushes, passed out, [the] next morning.*
> *Kerry: Alive or dead.*
> *Theresa: Or both. It was known for going all night long. It would start at dark-thirty, or 7:09. People would wander in and out, and then all the musicians and entertainment people would come after hours and that would keep it going. Before you knew it, it was sunrise. But it was also huge—close to four hundred people throughout the night. Money would come from T-shirt sales, and we had to put that [cash] in a secure spot. We would take the doorknobs off the bedroom doors so nobody could get in. One of the Savages' propmeisters fashioned handles out of corncobs and attached shafts. We would carry these in our pockets as keys to get in, and the bedroom was the only place that had air conditioning. So we would go in there to cool off, take the money in and just kind of refresh a little bit.*
>
> *One year, this whole batch of bikers came in. I was the only one there. Everyone else was out picking up trash up and down the street. I came*

Third Annual

Shrovinover's Sagittariad

December 3rd, 1977   ©tommybee   Corn Palace

The archer wore a fez as he galloped into gaiety.
Courtesy Tommy Bauman.

out of the bedroom, and there were these guys, these huge bikers. I'm like, "Well, hello." They asked if we had any beer, and of course, we did. But they made us give them all our beer just to go away. They asked what was behind the door and why was it locked, and they had this really beefy biker girl who was edging in way too close for me. It scared the crap out of me. It was ugly and tense.

Artly: We went through ten or twelve kegs a night. It got too big. Free beer, free music. Word of mouth would go out. It had been going on for fifteen years. Everybody had told everybody. We never had to advertise. There were a lot of drugs in those days.

Kerry: It started small, then got out of control. [21]

A sub-happening was the Shrovinover's Saggitariad, a celebration of birthdays under that sign—especially Tommy B's—held in early December. The event occurred sporadically over several years, beginning in 1975. An explanation of the odd name and the odd number comes around in the Uranium Savages section, just a few pages away.

5

PUMPKIN STOMP

J im Franklin was born in Galveston in 1943 and raised in La Marque, both coastal towns in southeast Texas. He knew by the second grade that he would be an artist. Franklin came to Austin in the late 1960s, having studied at the influential San Francisco Art Institute during the Haight-Ashbury heyday of rock 'n' roll dance concerts and their posters. One of his first ventures was opening the Vulcan Gas Company at 316 Congress. It became the city's first serious original music venue that promoted psychedelic and blues bands and that featured a light show. It was for one of the performances that JFKLN (his pen name/logo) drew his first armadillo. When the Vulcan closed, he moved with other entrepreneurs to start the Armadillo World Headquarters in August 1970. JFKLN was named the music hall's artistic director and was responsible for an amazing array of surreal murals, wall decorations, paintings on canvas, gig posters, handbills and signs.

Franklin also managed the Ritz on Sixth Street for about a year when Esther's Follies operated it. Here is how JFKLN explains the last rain of pumpkins:

> *The Stomp originated in Houston at the Love Street Light Circus and Feelgood Machine* [a psychedelic nightclub] *with Ramon Ramon and the Four Daddyos. It was during Halloween, and we were in an old school bus. We stopped at a pumpkin stand on the way down to Houston, and we stopped at a convenience store where I got about six cans of tomato soup and a knife. I precisely cut the stem and lifted it out, then poured in the soup. The seeds inside really work with the soup*

to look grizzly. I also made a slit on the side so that the pumpkin would break easily.

At the show, I placed some plastic trash bags on the stage, and I put the pumpkins on the stage. We had the upper torso of a female mannequin, bald, with hand-drawn nipples. She was sort of the band's mascot, Newnie. I threw a big plastic bag over my head, which came down to my knees, and placed Newnie upside down under the sack facing outward between my legs. I told the band to play "Rumble" or something that menacing. Ramon Ramon and the Four Daddyos [were] P.J. McFarland on drums, Ike Ritter on guitar, Ted Nicolo on guitar and vocals, Blank Mercer on vocals, Bill Dorman on bass and me on tambourine and bullshit.

It worked. I come out in slow motion and straddle the pumpkin, then the head [of Newnie] comes down and touches the pumpkin, gently at first, then progressively harder. Finally, because of the previously made cuts, the head penetrates the pumpkin. Then I tipped it upright and stepped back. It looked like the mannequin was wearing a pumpkin helmet, with streams of seeds and tomato soup stringing down. It was alive, moving.

After the song was over, I picked up Newnie and carried her over to the go-go dancers' stand on one side of the stage. So she was on display for the rest of the set. Then I brought her back [to Austin] with us on the school bus.

A couple years later, the Dillo booking agent asked me for a suggestion, and I said let's do a Pumpkin Stomp and get back together Ramon Ramon. Greasy Wheels was kind of the steady house band. They were going to open. It was the largest crowd we'd had in those first three years. A line to get in stretched around the block. They knew what to expect. It was the hip thing to do. You were too old to trick-or-treat in the neighborhood. There were also frat parties, but we basically made Halloween into a ritual. A ritual is nothing more than the public display of sacred secrets. After that night at the Dillo, Ramon Ramon got booked at Soap Creek.

There was a guy named Iron Feather, a great character who had a penchant for guns, and who, in this case, had a smoke grenade, and he asked me permission to detonate it in a washtub when we did the Pumpkin Stomp [at the Ritz]. And I said no, no—we don't want to do that, not in a theater.

I envisioned preparing the whole town, basically, for this. It would have to be organized. If it's done in a room, you can kind of educate the room. When you've got a street full of people and try to get the full street to chant, to join in this absurdity, that was part of the deal. I had a pile of

41

The Pumpkin Stomp enjoyed a long run at several venues. *Courtesy Jim Franklin.*

pumpkins, a ladder with a platform on top, and about an eight-foot climb. I wore my high gear: deer antlers, black felt hat, Texas flag on my chest with a black choir robe, and my armadillo crown—quite an image. That was my standard high priest gear. People thought I was about to form a cult. This was the period of time when cults were happening around. I wasn't about to do that. Instead, I was a sort of cult-iclast, trying to break them down. But it was a tease. It worked really well on the Pumpkin Stomp and fueled attitudes about what I was up to. I would call for a pumpkin. We put a pan with water and dry ice so that a vapor came over the top of that ladder.

What happened on the marquee of the Ritz was really a learning experience. You can't do a theatrical thing in a milling crowd. The fellow did bring his washtub and [set off] the smoke grenade. It was out on the platform, but the smoke drifted into the theater, and the few people who were inside to see the show we had going, but as soon as the smoke came in, they left. Word got to the fire department that smoke was coming out of—or actually going into—the Ritz. By the time they got there, it was already gone because it was controlled smoke. I hadn't wanted the guy to do it, but he had a good party spirit. He had an edge to be a little bit crazy. Not insanity crazy, just daring and out there. That was the last Pumpkin Stomp.[22]

Jim Franklin (far left) and other luminaries sample the snacks at a South Austin Popular Culture Center art opening. *Author's collection.*

Afterward, the Austin police put barricades up the middle of Sixth Street and made people walk around in one direction, an idea the police got from Dallas. The controlled aspect of Halloween persisted for many years but has been recently relaxed. Later in this volume, the Uranium Savages (one of the performing bands) add their remembrances of that fateful night.

Jim Franklin continues to produce great paintings and drawings for events and exhibits in Austin. His beard might be white these days, but his hand remains deft and his vision keen.

6

SPAMARAMA

David Arnsberger came from Houston to Austin in 1972 to study anthropology at the University of Texas. As it turned out, he ended up spending more time drinking beer than doing homework. During one particularly dreamy evening at the bent elbow, he and his friend Dick Terry were musing on the prevalence of chili and barbecue cook-offs. The too-frequent contests seemed silly to this pair and not very challenging. What about a way to make Spam[23] palatable? A Spam-off would be a worthy trial. Let's call it Spamarama!

The much-reviled pink canned lunchmeat originated in 1937, manufactured by the Hormel Foods Corporation of Austin, Minnesota. It received widespread use during World War II as a military ration and survival staple in such places as Russia, England and the Philippines. Depending on their history and under what conditions they used Spam, people either love it or hate it. To some, it's a welcome delicacy; to others, it's a kind of joke. The English comedy troupe Monty Python got tons of laughter from their parody about it, and naming unwanted e-mail after it doesn't help its reputation.

Spamarama, aka the Pandemonious Potted Pork Festival, began on April Fool's Day 1978 (a Saturday) at the original Soap Creek Saloon. The Uranium Savages, the crazed Austin parody band detailed in a later chapter, included David Arnsberger as an occasional member. We pick up the story from Awn and the Snuffs:

Kerry: Savages were the first band to play it, at Soap Creek. It was out in the club's backyard during the day. It had six entrants. Then it got bigger every year, then real super-big. Then Hormel found out about it. They were all pissed off because we were making fun of Spam. They came down here and caused a stink, and there was a bunch of trouble. Hormel ran it one year, but it was a complete flop.

Artly: There was a Spam Olympics and a Spam Toss. With a lot of Spam on the ground, dogs would go eat it. It looked like dog food and was to many people. Hormel didn't like that image.

Theresa: It was diluting their product, a legal term for harming it. They had no clue. They didn't get the whole concept, that we were making fun of Spam. And we were, but in a nice way.

A: And giving them publicity. It had a real Austin flavor, with collectible posters and collectible T-shirts.

K: Sales of Spam that week spiked in Austin. But it got too big. It imploded. Tried it in Boulder and Dallas, but it wasn't quite the same. It never caught on.

The festival endured several years at the original Soap Creek {What was that address?[24]} before moving with the saloon to a couple other locations and then to such venues as Scholz Garten, La Zona Rosa, Auditorium Shores, East Sixth Street, the Cedar Door and Waterloo Park. Other musical acts besides the Savages played, including the Booze Brothers, Parrot Lounge Orchestra, Rotel and the Hot Tomatoes, Kinky Friedman, Austin Lounge Lizards and Steven Fromholz, often all together in a Spam Jam.

The almost-palatable contest entries ranged from Spam ice cream and Spambrosia to Spamchiladas, Spamgator Gumbo, Spamalama Ding Dong, Piggy Paté, Spamalini, Guacaspamole and—believe it or not—Chicken-Fried Spam with White Gravy. Many of these dishes were outstanding enough to be included in a cookbook that the promoters published to commemorate the first twenty years of Spamarama.[25]

Every cook-off needs judges, and this pasty porkish party suckered some of Austin's most outstanding celebrities to sit on the panel. They ran the gamut from political figures such as agitator and former Texas agriculture commissioner Jim Hightower and former city council member Max Nofziger to media personalities from radio and television stations (Bob Cole, Joyce and Mel and Mary Vance) and humor columnists like John Kelso (who had plenty to write about from his experiences sampling, including an admonition to not) to real foodies such as Eddie Wilson, David Spooner and Chef John Myers. Coveted prizes in both open and professional divisions were best and worst taste, showmanship and the ultimate Spamerica's Cup. The above-hinted-at mayhem known as Spamalympics grew to encompass a relay race, Spam Call (like a hog holler) and Spam Cram (how much can you eat?).

The whole hog was finally canned, alas, by the year 2007.

7

HELMS STREET HALLOWEEN

Just to the south of Austin's Hyde Park lies the North University neighborhood. Formerly the dwelling place of college professors, it's now mostly condos for student rental. However, a few big and venerable structures remain. The present quietude of the streets, however, belies the wildness that went on there in the 1970s.

On the corner of Thirty-second and Helms Streets rises a large, late nineteenth-century squarish home. It's unusual because of its lofty center and four half-hip gables projecting in all directions, making three stories total. It comprises more than three thousand square feet altogether. The tower is an octagonal shape with four windows, each facing a corner of the house instead of a side. Zillow lists six bedrooms. A round Austin Landmark medallion graces the front porch because of the house's unique design and age.

If you'd been living in Austin in the 1970s and had run with a certain crowd, you'd have gotten wind of a big party coming on Halloween at the house on Helms Street. If you had happened to show up in your costume on October 31, 1977, a Monday night, you would have certainly looked askance at the fellow working the door. He was clad in a Smokey the Bear ranger felt hat bearing a gold badge, government-issue pants with a stripe up each leg and a matching uniform-style shirt with epaulets, buttoned pocket flaps and a Texas Youth Commission arm patch. He carried a realistic-looking pistol in a holster and a nightstick. You wonder, Since when does Helms Street need police?[26]

Right: The Helms Street house appears thusly from the south. Every castle needs a tower room. *Author's collection.*

Below: Halloween seemed more haunted in the house on Helms Street. *Author's collection.*

You wander in and avail yourself of a beer from the ice-filled washtub and some snacks laid out on a table. Choices include chips, pretzels, nuts, cookies, crackers, veggies and various sauces. Uproarious laughter erupts from the structure itself, so you make your way inside. You're impressed by both the haunted feeling of the house and the alternative lifestyle obvious to the place. Adjacent to the back door is the kitchen. Beyond that lie the big living room, entrance and stairway. You do a quick loop around this space and then venture up the wooden stairs to the second floor. This level consists of four big dormers, which seem to shrink the space the farther up you go. Here are four of the six bedrooms. Each is inhabited by different tenants and thus is distinctly decorated. Black light posters dangle in several places, and folks are everywhere hanging out in their various costumes, if they're wearing anything at all.

Up another steep and even narrower flight of stairs, you enter the tower room high above the yard. Inside this enlarged cupola you find more merrymakers and sweeping views of the neighborhood. The University of Texas tower, though not orange for the evening, gets framed nicely through the southeast window.

Across the whole property through stereo speakers blasts the Grateful Dead's new album, *Terrapin Station*. Even though its music's theme has nothing to do with the holiday, the orchestral strains will forever remind you of that madcap night.

Actually, there is a connection. The structure's current occupant is a woman-owned business called Red Fan Communications, a public relations firm. The first song on the album's second side is "Lady with a Fan." Only in Austin would anyone take notice of such a coincidence.

8

BALCONES FAULT

Question: who's to blame when eight excellent but wacky musicians appear onstage together in front of an amped-up audience? Answer: it's all Balcones Fault.

Fletcher Clark, a guitar player and economist who grew up in San Antonio, found himself unexpectedly living in Austin in March 1972. Just as unintended, he was suddenly appointed business manager at the Armadillo World Headquarters. While he oversaw construction of the club's new beer garden out back, he and his hometown friend Jack Jacobs began playing informal gigs before the evening shows. They needed a band name, so Eddie Wilson, one of the Dillo's founders, for five dollars came up with Balcones Fault.[27]

Geologists will recognize the term as describing an escarpment running through the middle of Texas, separating the Coastal Plains from the Hill Country. The abrupt change in elevation varies from two hundred to five hundred feet of altitude and accounts for major habitat differences. In Austin proper, it also precipitates a diversity of landscapes and—by association and extension—the profusion of people and their attitudes. {What does the word *balcones* mean?[28]}

The band remained an occasional duet or foursome for a time until Clark and Jacobs met Michael McGeary, who'd just drifted in from Hollywood. McGeary had long been a professional West Coast musician (briefly the drummer for Iron Butterfly), but it was his improvisational theater ingenuity that caught Clark and Jacobs's attention. Thanks to

McGeary's connections, five other multi-instrumentalists were soon on board. What began as an opening act for bigger names soon packed the halls as the headliner.

To attend a Balcones Fault performance at the Alliance Wagon Yard, Rome Inn or Armadillo World Headquarters was quite the party. At first the stage is dark, but slowly, a big cardboard rocket ship moves in from the wings, propelled by eight pairs of stockinged feet—no two alike—showing beneath the craft. The ship suddenly collapses revealing the troupe clad in nothing but colorful boxer shorts and socks. A couple of wardrobe girls from Esther's Follies come out and proceed to costume the members in all manner of gaudy pants and shirts and hats. The musicians take up their instruments and begin playing.

If you went to a Balcones Fault taping for the *Austin City Limits* (*ACL*) television program in the original studios in what was then the "big rusty building" at the corner of Guadalupe and Twenty-sixth Streets, you would have entered from the plaza floor and ridden the elevator to level six. In the lobby, you could get a cup of Lone Star Beer and then find yourself a seat in the U-shaped bleachers. Two floors above you soars the ceiling, and grids of spotlights, floodlights and fill lights illuminate the audience and the stage. The backdrop is a downtown Austin skyline drawn in realistic detail. It gives viewers back home the notion that *ACL* takes place outside. The backdrop was periodically updated as construction changed the cityscape. If you looked extremely closely, you could see a person's silhouette waving at you from a tiny window.

What impresses you most is the variety of styles that this ensemble cranks out. First might be a bluesy tune about a fellow getting suckered into cleaning a pretty woman's house only to find out she's married. The horn section, consisting of Kerry Kimbrough on trumpet and big Don Elam on a big baritone sax, honks the pulsating beat while Riley Osborne tinkles the ivories boogie-woogie style. McGeary is the lead singer for "I Got Fooled," but almost everyone else in the band takes a turn on vocals throughout the night, as well.

Next comes a slow, romantic ballad ("Waitin' on You") followed by a piece of pure funk ("Cold Cold Winter). Between songs, Jacobs throws out "We give you a little Colombian during the show, and you can give us a little Colombian after the show," a reference not to coffee. Then the band launches into a couple of South American cumbias and rancheras, which Jacobs delivers in excellent Spanish. People in front of you get up and dance, and you join them.

When, during lulls in the music, a juggler named Turk Pipkin rises up and keeps all manner of objects in the air simultaneously, a trained dog act (Clark McDermott and the Cold Nose Five) takes center stage, magician Harry Anderson causes a hapless band member to disappear and the infamous Chastity Fox writhes and contorts in a skimpy outfit, you begin to doubt that vaudeville is dead after all.

After another costume change comes a rousing rendition of Forty-second Street, complete with Charleston steps, sound effects and a simulated taxicab ride. Michael Christian, one of the drummers, delivers the lyrics with Jacobs. Elam now blows into his clarinet, and Kimbrough's trumpet gets a corny mute. Three guys wag their index fingers and alternately clap to the rhythm. In fact, every fellow in the band is high stepping. You'd think that Busby Berkeley had returned from the grave.

Throughout the evening, you're impressed by the excellent choreography, well-coordinated personnel switch-ups, superb musicianship and engrossing two-way audience interaction. It's a truly shared experience, especially when half the attendees are on their feet. When the giant inflatable banana hits you in the cranium, you bat it upward again.

Reviving another old-fangled era, next comes a Fats Waller medley, introduced with funny accents in unison by Jacobs in a miter and Christian in a fedora. McGeary relates what he likes about you, followed by Clark, who declares the joint is jumpin'.

Country music fans at your elbow aren't disappointed when the band nasally whines for you to not wait up for them tonight. Who could resist two-stepping to that? The relative calm gets shattered by Randy Newman's bawdy "Leave Your Hat On." This ditty involves dueling instruments, with guitars and sax and trumpet battling to overcome one another by fantastic ad-libbing and improvisation. Lead McGeary conducts these proceedings. Yes, he knows what love is.[29]

Austin's upstart show band of the mid-1970s, Balcones Fault knew how to please a crowd. *Courtesy Cream Records.*

If you'd gone to a Balcones Fault engagement any night near a full moon, you would have participated in the Moon Howl Minute, the precursor to a Full Moon Show. This involved the audience in a wolf-like chant for an entire sixty seconds, a frequent ritual that helped cement the connection between stage and hall. Jacobs's interest in mysticism and planetary influence was behind this. Each band member was able to put his expertise and skills to good use: McGeary served as stage manager, Elam did all the musical arrangements, Clark kept an eye on the financial situation and the others wrote songs.

It would be remarkable if such a bunch of talented guys didn't enjoy adventures together offstage. Not to degenerate into ADTs (amazing drug tales) in this narrative, but some vague memory lingers about the time the band played in a city south of Austin and found themselves being pelted with peyote buttons, which they made good use of later. Or there were hints of a drive to Houston, where they stopped in a field and gathered grocery sacks full of mushrooms, also quite useful for several magic days after. Nor could we dismiss reports of a Hot Knives episode, where two machetes were heated red-hot on a stove or in a campfire. Wads of a certain herb or lumps of its resin vaporized almost immediately when pressed between such utensils, creating instant mass euphoria. Those were dazed nights.

After amazing success from the middle '70s, the group recorded an LP and hit the road, relocating to California and touring throughout the country. The band reached a kind of climax when it performed in front of some 300,000 ecstatic fans in New York's Central Park. That high turned out to be unsustainable, however, because the thing that was central to the band's fortune—the over-the-top versatility and variety—also proved its undoing. Radio stations, record labels and booking agents couldn't categorize it as any one genre. The group was almost impossible to buttonhole. By early 1978, Balcones Fault had disbanded. For its members, collectively, the party ended.

But not individually—Fletcher Clark writes songs and produces albums; Michael McGeary went on to found the Lotions, Austin's first reggae band, and runs a fine woodworking shop; Riley Osborne is a much sought-after keyboard sideman; Don Elam just returned to Austin; Jack Jacobs died unexpectedly in 2006; Kerry Kimbrough, not sure; Dean "Stimulus" Stinsmuehlen operates a plastering and stucco company; and bassist Michael Christian plays with different lineups.

9

INNER SANCTUM RECORDS

P atrick Helton singled me out recently at the opening of an exhibit about 1968, that great and terrible year, in the Bullock Texas State History Museum. He's the current owner of Inner Sanctum Records. Seeing him made me realize that the story of one of Texas's earliest independent record stores could be included in this book, especially because of the celebrations it spawned.

Later, I caught up with Joe Bryson, who founded the store more than forty years ago. A finer raconteur cannot be found, much less one as eager as Joe to relate his past.

After growing up in Corpus Christi—Sparkling City by the Sea, the Riviera of the Gulf Coast—Joe graduated from Ray High School in 1966 and immediately moved to Austin to attend the University of Texas and thus avoid the draft. He had had some experience on the radio before coming north and knew how to fix a transmitter and what to say on the air. One of his first jobs in the Capital City was at KUT, the campus radio station operated by UT's engineering department out of an old carriage house next to the science building. He became adept in the knowledge of recorded sound and in proper ways to reproduce it. These were portents of things to come.

In the summer of 1970, when Joe was still enrolled in the marketing section of the business school, a teeny record store called Phil's stood at the corner of Twenty-fourth and Rio Grande Streets just west of the university. One day in August, Joe and his friend Ashley had just gotten back in town from Hippie Hollow and stopped to purchase a couple LPs. The owner's wife happened to casually mention that they wanted to sell the store and move back to New York City. This came as a bolt of lightning out of the blue to Joe, who had been contemplating self-employment for some time. He recognized this as a chance to make something of his talents.

Begging and borrowing from family and friends, Joe scraped together the requisite $2,900 and completed the transaction. He was now a businessman who owned a record store. His first task was to come up with a name for the new establishment. Joe recalled an earlier episode with other friends, who had referred to their apartment bathroom as the "inner sanctum." He threw that idea out, and (oh, wow) the company was named.

The original hours of operation were noon to midnight to match the sleep cycles of the store's soon-to-be clientele.

Using leftover funds, Joe and his helpers bought wood and tools and built bins for the twelve-inch records. {How many grooves are there on a typical record?[30]} On the first day he was to open, he left a friend in the store and then drove south to San Antonio to a wholesaler and brought back stacks of wax. They finished outfitting the place at 9:00 p.m. and decided to throw open the front door right then. With Joe's most excellent stereo system cranked up insanely loud, they played Pink Floyd's "Grantchester Meadows" off *Ummagumma*. People driving by did double takes, stopped and came in. Receipts showed $143.52 that first night. Joe had a good feeling about all of this.

In an unexpected turn, the lease on the first location was to end suddenly on the last day of September. Joe had to move the entire contents into his small house and then scramble for a new site. Another buddy ran a pants store in the corner of a big, old house at the junction of Twenty-fourth and San Antonio Streets next to Les Amis Café. With only a little finagling and a bit more cash, Joe found himself moving into a front corner room of what was later called Bluebonnet Plaza at 504 West Twenty-fourth Street.

Joe got set up, erected psychedelic-style signs and experienced instant success. Aside from a brief downturn when Joe moved himself into the store and slept behind the counter, business went up and up. He was selling out almost every other day.

About three years into ownership, Bryson stopped getting his records from San Antonio and instead drove to Dallas to the major label warehouses. Hugely beneficial were the close relationships he developed with the foremost industry representatives. Joe made the buying trip about every ten days, completely filling his diminutive Toyota Corolla station wagon with heavy albums, promotional materials and cases of Coors beer. By its fourth year, the business could boast a cool million in sales.

Inner Sanctum offered more than just rock 'n' roll to the public. A section in the front of the building, Inner Sanctum Too, sold classical and jazz music records.

The same artists who painted the Austintatious mural on Twenty-third Street—Kerry and Rick and Tommy B psychedelically decorated the inside of Inner Sanctum, covering every available square inch with swirling designs. Rick's sister played violin while the artists worked into the wee hours. Otherwise, Mackintosh tube-type amplifiers and top-notch speakers provided exceptional sound.

Musicians such as Willie Nelson and Jerry Jeff Walker would come into the store frequently.

By the time Joe had moved the main record store to a larger room at the rear of the building, he'd become aware of the Inner Sanctum radio show from the 1940s. He made sure that the store's new portal was big and heavy and made an eerie, loud creak when opened. With the increased space, Bryson began hosting more in-store events and record happy hours.

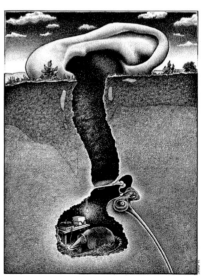

Inner Sanctum (IS) served as a one-stop shop of entertainment. You could audition records, buy records, buy concerts ticket and buy more records. You could linger for hours and blab, sort of like Cheers. Some of the big shows, such as the Rolling Stones, Grateful Dead and the New Orleans Jazz and Heritage Fest, offered tickets nowhere else. These sales were always only by cash—carloads of it. IS was also the exclusive outlet for *Austin City Limits* tickets. It was Joe who suggested to the TV show's producers that they provide beer to their patrons, a good move that survives into the present.

Every Friday around 4:00 p.m. was record happy hour with a keg of free ale. Artists would be present, signing albums. Robert Palmer, Joe Jackson

Inner Sanctum Records displayed an iconic Jim Franklin image on its promotional materials. *Courtesy Joe Bryson.*

and the Ramones became the store's friends. Mad Dog and Beans, famed for its huge, half-pound burger called the Bovine, was just around the corner. Joe Ely performed "Down on the Drag" from a stage out in the parking lot. That would have been around the time of the song's debut in 1979. Doug Sahm did another Austin anthem, "Groover's Paradise," at an in-store event. The cover art for that album features an intricate Kerry Awn drawing of a jumble of Live Music Capital icons, with the center image being that of IS's building. Sahm also recorded commercials for the store. Staff held look-alike contests with both Elvis Costello and Joe Jackson, with the latter serving as a judge for his. Robert Palmer showed Bryson the first Walkman cassette player he'd ever seen. Palmer performed live using instrumentation provided by that machine, mixed on the spot. The place was just packed. Psychedelic Furs, Toots and the Maytals—the pattern was set for other music outlets to do the same, even to this day.

How many other record stores could claim beer-soaked carpet on the floor? What other music retailer can brag of a sitting governor, Ann Richards, as a frequent customer with a penchant for heavy metal?

The biggest blowout was for IS's fifth anniversary on August 28, 1975. Bryson rented Lake Austin Lodges, a small resort that stood in a then-remote area west of town on the north shore of the river. Lone Star Beer donated fifteen kegs for the thousand invited people. At least half again that many showed up. LBJ's favorite caterer provided one thousand plates of barbecue dinners. Revelers drove cars or sailed boats to get there. They saw a three-foot-diameter birthday cake decorated like an LP and a bikini-clad girl pop out. One fellow came by whirlybird helicopter. That turned out to be crucial, as we'll see. The pilot ferried folks in and out most of the day, lending a *M.A.S.H.*-like air to the proceedings. Bands such as Steam Heat, Diamond Joe and the Dynamos and the (no surprise) Uranium Savages played.

By midnight the beer—both in the keg and in bottles—was almost gone. George Majewski, owner of Soap Creek Saloon, was in attendance, having shut his place down for the evening to be part of the crowd. Joe requested a couple of kegs from George, who easily consented. The two rode the helicopter several miles over the hills to the Saloon off Bee Cave Road in Westlake, coming to rest in the pot-holed parking lot. They duct-taped two kegs onto the patient stretchers on either side of the machine and attempted to take off. They just barely cleared some trees but did make it back to the party, dodging power lines all the way. As they made the approach to land, the pilot turned on a big bright search light, which shone down on the scores of remaining celebrants, who by then had cast off their clothes. Townsend

Miller reported on the party the next day in the *American Statesman*, naming it the event of the year.

As a climax of Joe's involvement just before he passed the torch to a new owner in 1982, the store received a much-needed spiffying. Bryson and one friend cleared the entire space, moving all the shelves and their tons of contents out to the parking lot over the span of one night. Above the merchandise, he suspended a parachute that resembled a big-top tent and held an extravaganza entitled Joe Bryson's Rock and Roll Circus Sale. This went on for three days around the clock. Twenty-seven bands played over that time period with Bryson costumed as the ringmaster. Employees dressed as clowns and operated a snow cone machine and a dunking booth.

By this time, the Dillo had closed, the record industry was changing and things weren't the same. The Cosmic Cowboy scene settled down somewhat, and Austin was beginning to be a nexus for punk rock. Again, the record store played a prominent role in purveying that style and its creators.

"Our mission was to stir the shit, cure boredom, and strip the gears of musical privilege in Austin, represented by the folk, blues and cosmic-cowboy oligarchies," wrote Huns drummer Tom Huckabee.[31]

Inner Sanctum won the *Austin Chronicle*'s Best Record Store award the first year, and Waterloo Records—which shared some key personnel with IS—has won it every year since.

IS celebrated a fortieth reunion at the North Door on East Fifth Street in 2010. Extreme Heat (heir of Steam Heat) and the Uranium Savages played, thirty-five years on. Bryson, now known as Condo Joe, runs a successful real estate company.[32]

10

LES AMIS CAFÉ

Over time, as things become more prosperous and safe, they become less peculiar and interesting, and that's evident [at] *no place more than here.*[33]

People in any sized city need a place to go that isn't home and that isn't the office. Such a "third place"[34] is vital to community cohesion. It benefits the individual by providing a social context; it helps the greater good by providing a stage where residents engage with one another to talk about politics, ideas and art on a mostly egalitarian basis. The casual nature of a third place puts folks at ease and encourages self-expression. It also cements a neighborhood's identity.

Such a site almost cannot be created but must develop organically. The correct mix of elements needs to be present: walkable location with a view of passersby; visible patrons who are as much on display themselves as are pedestrians; ease of accessibility; comfortable furnishings, variously sized seats and tables; simple and inexpensive fare; quiet atmosphere for conversation but not so quiet as to discourage it; a legitimate "right" for people to be there for hours at a time; reading matter and possibly games; and a local, frequent and regular clientele.

As a progressive and community-minded, medium-sized city, Austin can claim a few worthy street cafés. Foremost was Les Amis, located just west of the University of Texas campus where Twenty-fourth Street met San Antonio Street, in the same building as Inner Sanctum Records. Begun on a shoestring in 1970 by some guys as a place "to watch girls," Les Amis was part of a node of activity on that corner. Nearby was a used clothing store; Whole Earth Provision Company, which sold backpacks, hiking boots, and canoes; Mad Dog and Beans, a rumpled but popular joint to get a mondo hamburger; Pipes Plus, for all your smoking needs; and Smoothie King for refreshing fruity beverages. West Campus, long known as the "Student Ghetto," was in that direction, so scores of young folks walked or skateboarded past this corner every day and night. Like no other spot, this was Austin's answer to Haight-Ashbury.

Les Amis itself was nothing fancy: Wire spools made the tables, the ground was uneven and few chairs matched. Coffee was popular, of course, but so were the cheap beer and wine. The roof was of soft canvas. A short white picket fence separated the business from the sidewalk, and several trees and shrubs provided shelter and coziness. Almost no decorations enlivened the walls, but the restroom graffiti was unmatched anywhere else in Austin. Students, professors, artists, band members, filmmakers, screen- and other writers, hippies, cosmic cowboys and bohemians loitered there and nursed their drinks and smokes for protracted spans of time. The longer you stayed, the more likely you were to see someone you knew walk by or stop in. You chatted with friends or enjoyed solitude with no hassle.

The staff were notoriously nonchalant and eccentric, graced with youthful idealism, nihilism and humor. They, too, were just as content as the patrons to simply hang out, drinking and lounging. Casual doesn't even begin to describe their unhurried, almost apathetic attitude. They were between other jobs or other studies and had discovered their place in the scene.

Les Amis enjoyed a starring role in the film *Slacker*, which portrayed Austin's laid-back lifestyle of the late 1970s. Director Richard Linklater was a regular at the coffee shop and also lived around the corner. He expertly captured on film the café's atmosphere and vibes as well as its peeps. Ironically, the slacker lifestyle was coming to an end about the time the movie got widely viewed.

Although Les Amis was in many ways like a slow and quiet circus, it on one occasion hosted an organized celebration. If you'd been there on December 3, 1988, you would have just returned to the neighborhood after hearing some punk music in a city nightspot, such as Raul's, Club Foot or Muther's. But because several musicians and singers worked at and frequented Les Amis, that night was a good one to hear Tom Smith and the Dogshit Rangers. They were loud and boisterous. Tom, as lead singer, had stripped off his shirt and likely would soon strip his vocal cords with all his yelling. Patrons were whipped into a frenzy.

After twenty-seven years of casual wildness, Les Amis closed in 1997, a victim of skyrocketing taxes and the owner's plan to renovate the aging building. Mad Dog was gone, as well; Inner Sanctum was but a shell of its former self; the nearby Varsity movie house {What remnants of the former theater still exist?[35]} had converted to a group of small shops; and the once-cheap West Campus area was overrun by condomania. The city's population was booming, and new high-rises ascended downtown. The staff was supremely disappointed to have to abandon what had been a second home for most of them, and they expressed no small amount of bitter dismay about the decision. But the final party on the last evening of business was one for the record books. Staff members were literally hanging from the rafters. Times they were a-changin', yet the communal spirit of Les Amis lives on elsewhere, as we'll discover.

Not surprisingly, the Starbucks that replaced Les Amis provides nothing of these "third place" features, only predictable and expensive coffee beverages. No one goes there to plan the next insurrection.

PART II

YEARLY BLOWOUTS

11

CARNAVAL BRASILEIRO

One of the aspects of living in the Live Music Capital of the universe is not just the quantity of tunes available to folks here but the variety as well. On any given night, one can likely find the expected rock, folk and Americana styles. What's perhaps not so surprising is to also discover Irish, Middle Eastern or Jamaican bands. But would you believe you can also stumble on Brazilian?

Sure, a fair number of people from Brazil live here, but the catalyst behind one of the world's biggest eruptions of Rio-style pre-Lenten song and dance outside South America was a group of homesick students who were in Austin on Fat Tuesday 1975 for an intensive English course. They missed their usual celebration, so these two hundred restless mortals decided to create their own.

From that humble beginning, the event grew, not just because of native Brazilians, but also thanks to an on-air personality at a college radio station. KUT is the National Public Radio affiliate at the University of Texas at Austin. The station features block programming, which means that one show is likely to convey a completely different theme from its predecessor or successor. An array of themed shows happens daily and nightly each week, covering such diverse genres as Texas music, jazz, folk, old Rockabilly, alternative, ambient and blues. Every Friday afternoon, the station broadcasts *Horizontes*, which features Latin American styles. At least one such program a month concentrated on the rich multiplicity of tunes and songs emanating from Brazil. One of the show's revolving hosts was Mike Quinn, who also worked in a record store and developed a fascination for collecting Brazilian music. He got involved with the early editions of Carnaval and, in 1978, found himself in a leadership position. His promotion of the event, both in person and on KUT, greatly expanded its growth. Carnaval's first official poster, drawn by local artist Micael Priest in a fanciful style reminiscent of those from San Francisco's 1960s rock concerts, soon appeared on trees, telephone poles and newsstands all around town.

As the number of participants increased, so did the event's elaborateness. Soon also, the party grew into large and larger venues. Palmer Events Center has been Carnaval's home since 2003.

If you arrive early, having bought your ticket online, you move past the Will Call window and into the spacious hall, scene of many other mega-sized Austin events, such as the Settlement Home Garage Sale, Armadillo Christmas Bazaar and the Texas Roller Derby. But now the huge room seems empty in its first half, except for a pizza vendor's booth. Toward the middle of the space stand two bleachers, one on each side. At the hall's front stands a stage that occupies the full middle third of the room's great width. A square area is marked off with yard-high barricades immediately in front of the stage. You take special notice of the cash bars on both sides of the room because you anticipate getting thirsty from all the physical activity to come. A strange and deep rumbling from behind walls hints that tumult will erupt soon.

The Austin Samba School steps from backstage. There seems to be several dozen of them, all clad in matching uniforms of white shirts and trousers with blue shackos {Which are?[36]} and white plumes. They carry a variety of percussion instruments, from snares and tom-toms to bells and shakers. The band is fronted by a group of dancers with similar costumes. It's all about the rhythm, which this bunch pumps out mercilessly, members swaying as they pound.

The theme for this year's installment is the movie *Black Orpheus (Orfeu Negro)*, the 1959 classic that began the bossa-nova craze in the United States in the early 1960s. The film casts the mythic Orpheus and Eurydice story in Rio de Janeiro during Carnaval. Elements, symbols and characters from the feature now inform the grand entry parade. You see Orfeu's streetcar, the tragic hero himself, his forlorn lover and the villainous Death as they strut into the big room. Songs and melodies from the movie, such as "Manha de Carnaval" and "A Felicidade" feature prominently all evening. By now, the arena is getting noticeably crowded.

Above: Carnaval
Brasileiro features a
percussion marching
band. *Author's collection.*

Right: Backstage,
Carnaval's pageantry
extends to its decorative
wall hangings. *Author's
collection.*

Main stage entertainments and floor shows come one after another throughout the night. You hear bands and soloists and wish you could understand Portuguese. The performers are top-notch, many of them from Rio itself and one of whom played in the movie. Colored lights flash and swirl all around the stage and into the room.

If you bought the VIP ticket or are lucky enough to know the producer, you attain access to a special area behind the scenes, the Samba Circle Lounge. There are tables of free snacks, photograph opportunities, posters from past Carnavals and a bit of relative quiet for relaxation. You use the opportunity to greet band members and to make small talk with other longtime revelers.

Perhaps more stunning than the official artists are the audience dancers and their costumes. Even though this festival happens in the Northern Hemisphere's winter, Austinites tend to wear very little when they attend Carnaval. You see lots of skin plus all the usual characters from fantasy and cartoon worlds. There's Captain America, the Tin Woodman and the gang from Sesame Street. Bolas, feathers, beads, body paint, glitter, tassels, masks and hats are the rule. Just like in the movie, everybody's gyrating to the infectious beat. It goes and goes and goes.

As the samba party's autobiography concludes:

> *Carnaval has emerged and thrived in Austin because long ago it became a city of open attitudes and spontaneity, due in large part to the university influence. Now that bohemian attitude has mixed with just enough business sense and hard work to make music happen in a way that is attracting attention from around the world. Perhaps the greatest monument to that spirit—the defunct Armadillo World Headquarters—is now just a memory. But Austin's Carnaval Brasileiro, our peculiar winterfest of flesh and fantasy, was nurtured in that unique semi-cohesive, culture-conscious environment, and still flowers every February.* [37]

12

SAINT PATRICK'S DAY

While not exclusive to the city of Austin, this venerable event comes off with our own twist here in Groover's Paradise. Close to the Vernal Equinox and to UT's spring break, St. Paddy's often also coincides with South by Southwest (SXSW).

Not far from the capitol, at the intersection of Guadalupe and Seventeenth Streets, sits the Dog and Duck. This is our town's closest approximation of a real British pub, with many of the same trappings: cozy seating, stained-glass windows, sloping floor, fireplace, mummy, dart board, tin ceiling, billiards and a wall of taps. Weekly pint nights {Which occur on which days?[38]} are

Lively tunes from the Capitol City Highlanders pipe band stir the blood. *Author's collection.*

All sorts of festive garb are appropriate on Saint Patrick's Day at the Dog and Duck Pub. *Author's collection.*

always fulfilling, and patrons enjoy the selection of authentic pub grub, such as fish and chips, shepherd's pie, bangers and mash and Scotch eggs. Billy Forrester was one of the founders, and he also opened the first brewpub in town, called Waterloo. This Dog and Duck shares its name with a real London one in Soho, where George Orwell took his pints.

Being Austin, we like to blend things. March 17 (same as the street) goes berserk at Dog and Duck, combining the purely English atmosphere with other Celtic expressions. Hence, beneath the Texas-sized green-striped tent top gather all manner of O'Rileys and O'Shaugnessys who lap up Guinness Stout and Harp Lager with MacPhersons and MacTavishes in their tartan kilts. They listen and step to Sean Orr and Black Dagger and to Ian McLagan and the Bump Band. They wear whimsical buttons that say, "Kiss me, I'm Irish" and try the Irish stew. Everybody cries when the singers lead "Danny Boy."

It's all free and starts in the afternoon, extending well into the evening. Faith and begorah!

13

OLD SETTLER'S MUSIC FESTIVAL

Y ou can stay inside the city limits and be busy celebrating every night, but other opportunities present themselves just a short drive away.

In 2014, the Old Settler's Music Festival (OSMF) gave its twenty-seventh annual iteration in central Texas. The fest began in 1987 in Round Rock, a small neighboring city to Austin's north, and got its name from a municipal park there. In the early years, the emphasis was bluegrass music, but over time its genres have included roots, Americana, folk and bluesy acoustic jazz. Situated near Brushy Creek, the stream that flows past the round rock that gave rise to the town's name, the fest experienced a flood in 1997. The high water caused considerable alarm, almost stopping the show and compelling the promoters to begin seeking higher ground elsewhere.

In 2000 and 2001, Old Settler's happened at Stone Mountain Event Center just west of Dripping Springs.[39] When that facility closed, the promoters discovered a more conducive site just outside Driftwood, Texas, a wide place in the road with more residents in the cemetery than alive. On the banks of Onion Creek stand Salt Lick Barbecue, the Salt Lick Pavilion and Camp Ben McCulloch.

One of central Texas's most legendary purveyors of wood-smoked meats, the Salt Lick has been in business since 1967. Its creator was Thurman Roberts, who began the enterprise as a hobby. Even though it's twenty miles from Austin, the restaurant attracts a consistent and loyal constituency. It has added numerous buildings over time to accommodate ever-growing groups of eager diners. More recently, it expanded farther, acquiring land on the other side of Onion Creek to build its Pavilion under a pecan grove, which offered space for weddings and other large, private events.[40]

Onion Creek is a unique stream in central Texas because it rises from springs in the Hill Country and flows off the Balcones Escarpment a goodly way before merging with the Colorado River downstream of Austin. The springs dripping in Dripping Springs form one of the creek's tributaries. Ranches line its upper reaches, but in Driftwood, its right bank forms the boundary of Camp Ben McCulloch. {Who was McCulloch?[41]}

Since the camp's founding, Confederacy-allied groups have met there up to modern times.[42] Even today, names of longstanding families are mounted

Above: Onion Creek's delightful current gives waders a chance to stay cool at Old Settler's Music Festival. *Author's collection.*

Opposite, top: Tabletops at Camp Ben McCulloch honor the memory of Confederate veterans. *Author's collection.*

Opposite, bottom: Engaged listeners get ready for the Sunday afternoon sets at Old Settler's. *Author's collection.*

on trees where they erect compounds year after year. In October, Camp Ben hosts the Austin String Band Festival, and the property is operated year round by a private association as a public picnic and camping place.[43]

In its current configuration, OFMF runs for four days, Thursday through Sunday, the second weekend of April. Campers arriving by the first night are treated to a lineup of five bands at the covered central stage. Friday and Saturday, the action shifts across Ranch Road 1826 to the Salt Lick Pavilion, where three major stages present concerts and workshops all day and up to midnight. During the two main days, commuters from Austin and other places swell attendance to the thousands. Sunday, Camp Ben is

Austin's archetypal armadillo found his way to Driftwood along Onion Creek. *Courtesy Jean Spivey.*

once again the center of activity, beginning with a gospel service in the morning and continuing with bands playing through 5:00 p.m.

While the entire history of OSMF is beyond the scope of this writing, it's handy to regard any large festival as a collection of smaller parties. As happens during many other outdoor events, groups of people ally themselves and form recurring camping clusters, often pitching tents in the same spot every year. Some of these temporary tribes frequent several fests throughout the year but might change names at different locations. Eight-year festivalgoer Regan Brown explains:

> There's a lot of wonderful things about the campground. We have a camp called Camp Bona Fide, and we have a big one at Kerrville called Kerrfuffle. But this is a different group of friends. We call one another the "SemiAnnuals" because we come here for the Austin String Band Festival in October. It's a much smaller festival and very Kerrville. The campground's fun, and there's always a lot of great music.[44]

Another such group that gets extra involved is Team Goodtimes, which consists mainly of folks from San Marcos and Austin. This bunch claims its site on the western edge of Camp Ben between the paved road and Onion Creek. Group leader Cody Johnson has been attending since the early 2000s. Here's how he tells his story:

> On a particular Old Settler's, I was in an unusually ecstatic state of mind. Somewhere in the darkness one night, I came across a small fiddling circle that was playing the most beautiful, darkest, Gypsy-bluegrass-jazz that I'd ever heard in my life. I couldn't get quite close enough to listen, and some of the people around me were talking. I was thinking, wouldn't it be

A diverse array of portable housing styles provides temporary shelter at Old Settler's. *Author's collection.*

great if we had a place where no one was allowed to talk. The culture of Old Settler's at that time was a thousand campfire jams spread across the campground. And it was always awesome to wander through the night and into these different camps, but it was really the luck of the draw to find the really talented stuff that would really blow you away. You never know who's what, and there are no signs to tell you "Who is this? Who are you?" Sometimes weird little super groups are formed and what have you. That one where I went that night happened to be a culmination of some of the members of Green Mountain Grass and the Blue Hit.

I absolutely fell in love with those bands, and through that I was able to become friends and a part of this community of amazing, talented musicians. We kind of call ourselves the "Family." Coming from a place where these people were perhaps too young or not known enough to get recognition, even locally in Austin, Texas, to promote themselves, I felt we needed to make a space to showcase our friends' talents. That same year, Camp Ben had done some bulldozing of the site that would become Camp Goodtimes, and I jumped on it. They'd leveled the area and created a little natural amphitheater, so to speak. Probably taking it way too seriously, I'd gone out there months in advance to scout out the future site where my camp would be. Everything was perfect, and it looked like it was going to work. Even from high school, I'd always had a passion for throwing house parties as long as I could remember. I'd acquired a small stage, which I took out to Old Settler's to showcase the talent of my local Austin musicians.

That first year, 2007, I think we had just the Blue Hit play the first night [and] then Green Mountain the second. After the latter had finished, the whole crowd screamed for the Blue Hit. Grace [Park, the lead singer] was asleep in her tent on the other side of camp. She woke up, came out and played again. It was particularly cold that early morning, and I remember watching the fog come out of Grace's mouth as she sang. I stepped back for a second and felt like I was part of a party that had been going on for one hundred years. I remember thinking that this is how vampires party.

As a result of this initial success, we were able to do it every year, setting the bar a little higher each time. It's gotten to the point that I get e-mails from bands that I've never even heard of from San Francisco and Nashville who have heard of this little stage and want to play a set. Now that the momentum has picked up, I needn't tell people that I'm a nobody who runs an unofficial nothing in the middle of an actual festival, asking would you like to come play acoustically in the middle of the night when its freezing cold for a bunch of people under the influence talking and getting shushed for a free T-shirt. Somehow, we've been able to do it, which is awesome.[45]

Team Goodtimes presents outstanding bands after hours on its campground stage. *Courtesy Jean Spivey.*

Grace Park's experience encapsulates the singer-songwriter milieu that seems particularly prominent in the Austin metro area. Born in 1984, she grew up in Albuquerque and Marble Falls. She began her college career at Southwest Texas State, now Texas State University, where she studied radio and mass communication. She was attracted to the town's music scene and met and played in several local clubs such as Momo's. Grace completed a bachelor's degree in music performance and began attending Kerrville Folk Fest in 2006. There she met cellist David Moss and guitarist John McGee. Beginning early in 2007, they formed an acoustic trio that called itself the Blue Hit. They became known for late-night sessions in the campground of Quiet Valley Ranch, home of Kerrville Folk. Performing covers and some self-written songs, Grace stood out with her high, quavering soprano and fluid body movements.

Late in 2012, Park formed the Deer with bassist Jesse Dalton and guitarist Mike McLeod, both of whom she had met in "San Marvelous." Often utilizing other accompanying vocalists and instrumentalists, the Deer is a vehicle for Grace's original material. In that band, she also takes up the guitar, playing as she sings. A true multimedia artist, her original cutout paper artwork embellishes the Deer's CDs and website. The band plays in numerous coffeehouses and nightclubs and is accessible on YouTube videos.

Grace Park speaks of the situation from her perspective:

> [Goodtimes is] *a camp that's strictly for listening, and it's a really good forum for new music. I've heard a lot of good bands that stick with me through the whole year. Cody's a real good patron of the arts. You won't find him in the program, but he's a huge part of Old Settler's, at least for me and for a lot of people. A lot of people are annoyed by all the shushing. But you go into camp, there's a stage with a big light sculpture and everybody's gathered around, maybe two hundred people listening each night. If you're talking, you get shushed. They have to do that because otherwise if people just stand around and talk, nobody would be able to hear the musicians, and you wouldn't get to have the really good musicians who come to play that stage.*[46]

It's no secret that Cody Johnson built his Team Goodtimes stage to showcase the Deer and similar bands of their ilk (elk?). All sessions are field recorded.

Peculiarities of OSMF include the fact that it's but one weekend and barely an hour's drive from downtown Austin. As such, at least for the Austin-based

Clever construction attracts friends to Bamboozle Camp at Old Settler's. *Author's collection.*

campers, it doesn't feel like you've gone somewhere or really gotten away from it all. The folks from Houston, Dallas or places farther afield, however, hold a differing opinion. For them, the fest is much more of a pilgrimage. As we've noticed in the comments, campers and camp compounds become regulars, loyally attending year after year.

14

EEYORE'S BIRTHDAY PARTY

Perhaps the most iconic of all Austin festivals, Eeyore's was started in 1964 by a University of Texas fraternity member, Lloyd Birdwell, as a way to entertain sorority girls. Named for the dour donkey in the Winnie-the-Pooh stories, the party was first held in Eastwoods Park, which is just across the street from the north edge of campus and behind the home of folklore writer J. Frank Dobie. {What did he call the UT tower?[47]} With a forest-like feel, the park's a nine-acre public space with lots of trees, trails and picnic tables; a sports court; and swing sets. A branch of Waller Creek, the informal eastern boundary of Old Austin, forms the park's southern boundary. Costumes, beer, a birthday cake and a maypole embellished the party's first installment, and Lloyd and his friends decorated trees and tables around the park to add color to the festive atmosphere. The first year saw just a small group of attendees, but more and more folks arrived as the party became a much-expected annual affair. Soon, the UT English department got involved in the party's organization and execution, lending a scholarly air to the scene.

As the festival grew in size and popularity, young children began attending, as well. The original elements laid the groundwork of the fun that has endured these last fifty-plus years of celebration. Having seen fliers tied to trees on campus and hearing about the tomfoolery from friends, I remember attending in 1973. It was quite joyful, with people cavorting merrily about, and pretty crowded. With congestion and the need for more space, leaders sought some elbowroom.

A maypole has been part of Eeyore's birthday celebration from its first year, 1964. *Courtesy Jack's Party Pictures.*

The dour donkey in bronze marks the site of the original Eeyore's Birthday Parties in Eastwoods Park, just north of the University of Texas campus. *Author's collection.*

In 1974, Eeyore's moved to forty-two-acre Pease Park,[48] a bit farther from campus than Eastwoods and westward. Named for a former Texas governor whose mansion still stands up the hill nearby, Pease—pronounced "peace" by some, "peas" by others—Park straddles Shoal Creek, the informal western edge of the original 1839 city. {Why do nearby streets sound like Connecticut cities?[49]} Not only did the new site offer a larger stream along one border, but it also had sloping terrain on its other edge, a major greenbelt trail connection, and better visibility along Lamar Boulevard, Austin's longest street. {What was weird about Lamar?[50]} Grown beyond its founder's control, the gathering now looked to the university YMCA for management. The Y, in turn, spun off a smaller organization called Friends of the Forest, which made the event a benefit for area nonprofit organizations. Local vendors of food, beverages and T-shirts donated their labor and all net earnings to a revolving list of deserving groups. Costumes got more elaborate, a live donkey came for pictures and spirited contests added excitement to tradition.

Typically scheduled for the last Saturday in April with a rain date for the following weekend, Eeyore's is easily the quintessential Austin springtime blowout. It anchors the light, warm months as much as Halloween on Sixth Street secures the city's dark, cool season. Here's what it's like to attend:

An aging but safe school bus is ready to take costumed passengers to Pease Park for Eeyore's Birthday Party in April. *Author's collection.*

The first hint that the situation isn't exactly normal comes when you park your vehicle in a state garage at Brazos and Sixteenth Streets and stride up to a sign decorated with crepe-paper flowers. There awaits an old yellow school bus half full of revelers, most of whom already wear colorful costumes and many of whom carry a drum of some kind. As soon as that bus is full, it drives south, and another takes its place to wait. As the lumbering vehicle heads west, anticipation builds among the passengers. In several blocks, after more intersections, the bus turns onto Kingsbury and stops at the south gateway to Pease Park. You and the other fun-lovers get off and are immediately engulfed in a sea of strange dress, with amplified rock music pouring down from a stage up the hill on your left.

Making your way past rows of concrete picnic tables and the playscape, you encounter the two-rows-deep line of local food vendors selling ice cream cones, sausage on a stick, turkey legs, veggie wraps, fruit cups, corn dogs, cupcakes, smoothies and many others. If you don't pause there now,

The Capitol Building's Goddess of Liberty makes a rare appearance at Eeyore's Birthday Party. *Courtesy Dave "Sparky" Verrett.*

Celebrants can choose from all manner of food and drink at Eeyore's Birthday Party in Pease Park. *Author's collection.*

you continue up the gravel trail to the T-shirt booth to purchase this year's commemorative design or head just a few steps farther to the cash-out booth. There, you exchange dollars for little green tickets that are good for food or beverages. Next come the beer stands: Five tickets get you a pint cup full of ale or lager from a regional brewer. You can also purchase a glow-in-the-dark commemorative vessel, which sports Eeyore's cartoon image and the party's ordinal year.

A few steps and sips later, you behold the large open grassy space between the creek and the inclined wooded edge, and you wonder at the elaborate hats, body paint, masks, tutus, hula hoops and other outrageousness adorning the celebrants. A few dozen yards away stands poor sad Eeyore himself, wearing a garland of flowers, in a pen surrounded by children who want only to pet the donkey and to get their photo taken with him. Noting the line of all-important Porta-Potties on your left-hand side, you continue through the shade, careful not to step on folks' clusters of blankets or to trip over lawn chairs. A rhythmical throbbing gets louder.

There's just something primitive about the sound of a circle of drums, and the one at Eeyore's ranks as probably the best anywhere. If you're early, the circle is small or several are scattered about. By the early afternoon, though, it's probably grown to several hundred people. At the circle's nucleus are big bass drums, snares, congas, bongos and knockers, perhaps fifty in number.

A plethora of partygoers finds shady spots to gather and relax in Pease Park for Eeyore's annual celebration. *Author's collection.*

Inside them is a tight wad of dancers, who let the beat tell their bodies how to move. If you don't have a drum of your own, you can simply whack the bottom of your now-empty beer cup with your fingernails. Smoke of all kinds swirls around this fiercely free tribe, adding an air of euphoria.

No one person is the drum leader, but the pounding erupts organically from those present. Someone establishes a basic timing, and the others follow that. Gradually, the pace speeds up until it reaches a cacophonous climax, and everyone roars. Then the thrumming begins again at a different pace, slow or fast, and the entire cycle repeats throughout the day. Members of Austin's deaf community like the drum circle because they can physically perceive its loud pulsation.

You dance and pound as long as you like and then wander some more or get in line for the toilet. After that, you amble over to the playground to see the next generation of celebrants making good use of swings, merry-go-rounds and seesaws. On the sports field, you catch a glimpse of the egg relay race and egg toss and later linger for the spellbinding unicycle football game. You're not at all surprised to see Wavy Gravy in the park, either.

Eeyore's famous drum circle begins early in the day. *Author's collection.*

Robin Hood looks sharp in his early English regalia during Eeyore's Birthday. *Courtesy Dave "Sparky" Verrett.*

Above, left: Eeyore himself makes a thrilling appearance at his birthday party in Pease Park. *Author's collection.*

Above, right: "Tiger Drawers" Joe advertises for a mate during Eeyore's Birthday Party in Pease Park. *Author's collection.*

Back at the food booths, Jim O's stir-fry and Texas River School fajitas are mighty tasty, as is the Blue Bell ice cream. Another beer or two washes them down, and you hang out with friends talking about the day, the crowd, the costumes, political concerns and the next party. Stay in one place long enough, and you'll see Robin Hood, Batman, Silver Man, Half-Man, Green Woman, fairies, punks and shapely young women wearing nothing but paint.

It's a different experience if you volunteer for one of the vendors. Not only do established for-profit food trucks and other itinerant grub purveyors (such as Mr. Jim O') provide comestibles, but a few notable nonprofits set up ad-hoc shops as well. For more than fifteen years running, the Texas River School (TRS) has been serving scrumptious chicken fajitas to Eeyore's revelers. In keeping with the celebration's beneficent theme, this nonprofit

Marjorie Durst wouldn't dream of missing out on the wild times at Eeyore's Birthday.
Author's collection.

promotes its enterprise as a "FUNraiser" for its programs of keeping kids and rivers healthy.

During Eeyore's, TRS erects four or five pop-up awnings next to the Pease Park restroom with access to running water there. Out front, propped on sawhorses, are two red canoes on which are emblazoned the association's name. The booth, improvised with ladders, fabric and tables, offers food and beverages from two counters. On a propane grill nearby, cooks sear and roast the preseasoned chicken pieces. Sharp fellows cut them up, and folks in an assembly line place the meat with grated cheese and pico de gallo into flour or corn tortillas and then roll and wrap them in foil squares, ready for sale and consumption. In 2014, the team processed three hundred pounds of chicken, heated 1,275 flour tortillas and 240 corn ones, added 32 pounds of shredded cheese and 11 gallons of sauce and sold four hundred sixteen-ounce cups of lemonade. The booth's take amounted to more than $5,500.

The festival ends officially at dusk, but you're likely to be tired sooner than that. Your legs feel heavy from all that walking, and your mouth just cannot smile anymore. With great reluctance, you make your way back to the buses and board the next one out. Getting off at the parking garage, you bid a fond farewell to this installment of Austin's most renowned

Jim O's Fine and Fancy Foods booth always attracts an enthusiastic clientele at Eeyore's Birthday Party. *Author's collection.*

bacchanalia. Faithful attendee and ultimate social devotee Marjorie Durst said this after the 2014 affair:

So another Eeyore's has come and gone. Costume creation is a big part of the fun for me. It came together almost too easily this year. Forgotten phones and schedule mix-ups could have messed it up but didn't. Threats of rain may have kept a few away, but there were still plenty of painted bodies, animal costumes, feathers and craziness to go around. I love going when I'm ready and leaving when I'm done, having eaten, danced, hung out with friends and total strangers who may become new friends. Long Live the Blue Donkey!

15

O. HENRY PUN-OFF

Here we resume Will Porter's story.

In 1934, two decades after the short story writer's demise, the former Porter house was moved a few blocks to Brush Square, one of the city's original public parks, at Neches and Fifth (formerly Pine) Streets. Renamed the O. Henry Museum, it contains furniture, artifacts and compositions of the author. In addition, his name graces an entire room and collection in the History Center, the regional section of the Austin Public Library. Because of Porter's connection to this place, both in social life and in humorous literature, a group of funny Austinites initiated a pun-off in 1978 and staged it at the O. Henry Museum. Begun as a wholly local experience, today the pun-off attracts contestants from around the nation and has spawned similar events in other cities.

When you attend the free event in Brush Square behind the museum and its sister historic structure, the Susanna Dickinson House, on a sunny Saturday in May {What's the third museum in this same block?[51]}, you arrive early enough to find shade beneath the grove of live oaks on the east edge of the square, where you plant your blanket or lawn chair. Behind you are a couple of the ubiquitous food trucks that supply most of the city's festival meals. While listening to a whimsical band warming up the crowd from the centered small stage, you can't help but browse the book sale that's laid out on the right flank. In passing, you can glance at the registration table and only guess at what double-entendres the entrants will bring to the day, but surely most will make you double over.

Shady sod fills up first at the O. Henry Pun-Off in Brush Square, downtown Austin. *Author's collection.*

The first voice you're likely to hear after the music ends is that of intrepid wise-guy Gary Hallock, himself a former chortle champion, who has directed the hilarity since 1990. The performance platform makes Gary look even taller than his six feet, seven inches, and that American flag shirt he wears makes you want to salute him. He trades duties with the other emcees, Guy Ben-Moshe and Steve Brooks. Guy thanks the musicians and delivers a gag-spiked introduction to the impending word play. First question: what is a pun? He answers with a detailed definition and then invites the audience to say it back to him, a phrase at a time: "A pun is the humorous use of a word or words in such a way as to suggest different meanings or applications OR words that have the same or nearly the same sound but different meanings." With those criteria established, the show begins.

The pun-off consists of two sections. First comes "Punniest of Show," where some thirty-two contestants are each granted ninety seconds to deliver a prepared pun-filled monologue. They each do so, one after another, dredging up every imaginable topic from food to politics to romance, and you get sore from laughing. A panel of six judges, who occupy an awning to the left of the stage, rate each presentation on content, originality and general effect. Audience reaction is also taken into account when a judge numerically ranks an entrant by holding up a card. The louder you groan, the better a score. Totals are tallied on a big board to the right. In case of a tie, the crowd's applause cements the deal. After all contestants finish, you get to applaud the winner.

And the 2014 O. Henry Pun-Off winners are… *Author's collection.*

The second section is known as "Punslingers." This is an elimination round in which two funny folk vie against each other to play words on a random topic. The pair goes at each other until time or tongue runs out for one. The winner of each round faces the winner of a previous round, bracket-style, until a champion prevails. He or she gets a trophy and attendant fame.[52]

Insert your own worst joke here.

16

FLAG DAY

Jim Ellinger is a radio guy, community media nut and longtime notable denizen. He arrived in Austin from St. Louis in 1980 to produce an independent radio piece, *Last Dance at the Dillo*, during the final hours of the Armadillo World Headquarters. As happens to so many others, Jim succumbed to the city's allure and stayed on. For seven and a half years, he was a resident of Whitehall, Texas's oldest unaffiliated housing co-op, where lived older and less traditional students and nonstudents. Co-ops define much of Ellinger's life. For five years, he served as membership and public relations director of Wheatsville Food Co-op, the only grocery store in town, indeed in all of Texas, owned by its customers.

He's also been on and involved with Austin airwaves for probably four decades. His most conspicuous accomplishment to date was founding radio station KOOP-FM, an alternative noncommercial station that fills 91.7 megahertz with talk shows, music programs and news well outside of the mainstream.

When not jetting around the world to more than 250 cities in sixty-plus countries helping to start other community stations and cooperatives, Ellinger throws some intriguing parties involving plants, time and cloth. Jim lives on the northern edge of Hyde Park, mentioned earlier as one of the city's earliest suburbs. His house stands at a bend in the road across from a sizable traffic island, which sports grass, wildflowers, a streetlight and a couple trees. If you were walking by and peeked into the backyard, you'd see a tantalizing variety of bamboo breeds with many colors, thicknesses and heights. Jim is a member of Austin's branch of the Texas chapter of the American Bamboo Society. In that capacity, he helps folks clear out unwanted groves and to cultivate species that provide explicit utility, such as for privacy fences or poles. Additionally, Mr. Ellinger hosts gatherings of bamboo aficionados any time the society meets in Austin.

Like many other central Texas property owners, due to the mid-decade unrelenting drought and heat waves, Jim lost many trees in his residence and rental yards. He uses the opportunity of planting a new tree to host an irreverent "tree-planting ceremony," which involves quotations from everything from the Jewish Etz Hayyim to Druidism. Typical of multicultural Austin, there are usually about equal numbers of Hebrews and pagans at such an event.

Jim and his partner, Karen, do an annual blowout around the New Year. If you're invited and you walk up the driveway to the side entrance, you're immediately struck by his remarkable collection of signs that adorns the carport and the home's west wall. Guests to these events bring all sorts of drinks and covered dishes, and often sparklers and other flashy fireworks help scare away any demons.

Jim Ellinger's placard array continues to evolve. *Author's collection.*

Aside from strange placards, the other collection that takes up lots more of Jim's storage space is that of flags. An amateur vexilologist, he owns nearly two hundred banners from all over the world, from official governmental ones to the whimsical and fantastic. Indicative of his creativity and his contribution to Austin's offbeat nature, Jim has for thirty years headed up diverse installments of Flag Day. It's a bona fide U.S. commemoration on June 14, originated when the Stars and Stripes was officially sanctioned in 1777 and passed by congressional resolution in 1949.

Because it falls but a couple weeks after the better-known Memorial Day, Flag Day is often

Sometimes we just need a sign. This one hangs on Jim's back door. *Author's collection.*

overlooked—but not by Ellinger. While at Wheatsville in 1983, Jim's general manager assigned him the task of coming up with a promotional event quickly and on the cheap. No other civic or commercial organization had wrapped itself in Flag Day, so Jim jumped on it, hanging several dozen borrowed emblems around the store. The display generated a great deal of media coverage, with photos in the *Daily Texan* and the *Austin American-Statesman* and on a couple local TV news stations.

The next year, Jim gathered up a much bigger collection of flags, and the store was extensively blanketed with a wide variety of them. Almost everywhere, out of reach, there was a flag of some sort. This generated even more publicity, and Ellinger realized he'd birthed an important tradition.

After Jim left Wheatsville, he found space to arrange his collection in a prominent local coffeehouse, Ruta Maya, which touts fair-trade, organic beans. The display was another media attention–garnering success. It drew in customers, photographers and film crews. That continued until around 2001, when the shop moved. It was time for the idea to take on a new form.

Not every year, but otherwise consistently, Ellinger leads the city's smallest parade on or near Flag Day in his home neighborhood. If you had participated in this occasion recently, you would have met at Forty-fifth and Duval Streets at the Hyde Park Market, which itself boasts zillions of flags. As the small group gets ready, Ellinger offers plenty of extra bamboo poles and flags for folks who didn't bring either. After Jim's pep talk and briefing, the thirty-odd walkers cross Forty-fifth and stride up a couple blocks to Forty-sixth (Forty-five and a Half making the extra block). Around you are all ages of people carrying one or two flags of dazzling colors and sizes. Sometimes media outlets are present, and always several cameras capture the pageantry and exuberance. If neighbors are aware, they step onto their porches to cheer the procession.

Exuberant neighbors join the 2014 Flag Day Parade. *Courtesy Irene Tobis.*

After a couple more blocks, the miniature throng heads north onto the walk's final leg and reaches the spacious traffic island that fronts Ellinger's dwelling. An enormous Texas flag hangs from a string of electric lights over the pavement, and the troop runs twice around the island, cheering. After obligatory group portraits, everyone's beckoned to the backyard for soft drinks in the shade. When all are sufficiently cool, participants are awarded certificates in such categories as Best Kid's Flag, Best Non-National Flag, Most Colorful Flag, Most Outrageous Flag, Funniest Flag and enough others to give every marcher bragging rights. As is typical of just about every Austin gathering, you'd also enjoy the potluck snacks immediately following.

21st Annual Flag Day Celebration & Parade
Free! Fun! Flags!

Saturday, June 14th, 2014 6pm
Starting at the corner of 45th St and Duval St
ending at the corner of Fairfield Lane & Eilers Avenue

Jim Ellinger's 21st Annual

FLAG DAY
Celebration!

Flags a Flyin' in the
Austin Airwaves!

FINISH
Grassy circle at
Fairfield and Eilers

START
Hyde Park Market, Deli
and Organic Grocery

Austin's Biggest, Oldest,
Weirdest Flag Day Event!
Bring a Flag (free bamboo poles provided.)

Don't have a flag? We will lend you one!

Certificates and Prizes for
all sorts of categories of flags.

Make your own flag! A flag-friendly kid event!

Jim Ellinger sincerely hopes you can make his parade. *Courtesy Jim Ellinger.*

Vince Hannemann's Cathedral of Junk soars to dizzying heights above his backyard. *Author's collection.*

People of all colors turn out for the fun and frolic of Eeyore's Birthday Party. *Courtesy Dave "Sparky" Verrett.*

Austin's Graffiti Park, aka Baylor Street Art Wall, provides a colorful backdrop to many of the city's creative activities. *Author's collection.*

Only in Texas do longhorns substitute for bike handlebars. *Author's collection.*

Opposite, top: Maria Corbalan's bust beckons the hungry and the devout to her Taco Xpress. *Author's collection.*

Opposite, bottom: Each year's Skipper Pin entitled the wearer to discounts and freebees at the Austin Aqua Festival. *Austin History Center, Austin Public Library.*

SouthPop shows paintings, drawings and photographs from Austin's marvelous music milieu. *Author's collection.*

Invitation to celebrate despite poverty. *Author's collection.*

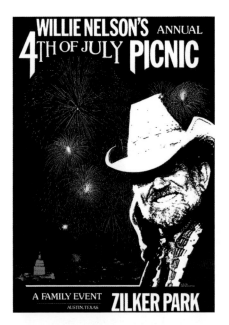

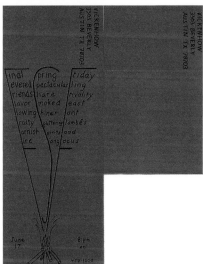

Clockwise from top left: Willie Nelson's 1990 blowout happened in Austin's Zilker Park. *Copyright ©
1991 Nels "Jagmo" Jacobson*; This party invited everyone from Corpus Christi who lived in Austin
in 1990. *Author's collection*; What could be more celebratory in spring than blossoms? *Author's
collection*; A narrow page enticed revelers to simmer in a Fire Song Focus. *Author's collection.*

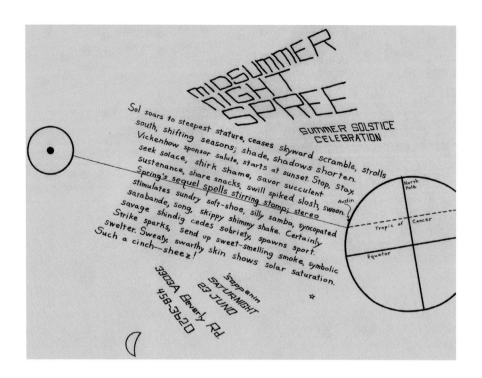

Above: Sibilance strained the searcher who scoped out a Saturday soiree. *Author's collection.*

Left: This was one of several public offerings of the 60s Marathon. *Author's collection.*

Opposite, top: Deceased musicians, artists, writers, public servants and roadies take their venerated place on the Memorial Wall at South Austin Popular Culture Center. *Author's collection.*

Left: A T-shirt image advertised Willie Nelson's 1975 Fourth of July Picnic in Liberty Hill, Texas. *Courtesy Jim Franklin.*

Right: Watchful Ear decorated the Corn Palace in the early 1970s. *Courtesy Tommy Bauman.*

Longest Day, Longest Affair

Celebrating Summer, Sun, and Fire

Four p.m.—Midnight
June 20, 2009
Saturday

HowLin host this block party at our neighbor's place across the street. Carol Kent's back yard connects with three other houses to create an enormous private park. You'll find a dance floor, fire pit, and gardens, the perfect setting for a steamy solsticial seasonal switch. Howie DJs the theme music programs. Please bring beverages or a dish.

Summer Sun Songs at 4, live band Road to Surfdom at 7, Fire Songs at 9, drum circle later 6400 block of Linda Lane, west side 627-4097 or 928-8485

Above: The vernal equinox of 2009 saw the world in mirror image. *Author's collection.*

Opposite, top: The 2014 Flag Day Parade ended with an obligatory group shot and potluck snacks. *Courtesy Irene Tobis.*

Opposite, bottom: The burning season, a nearby star and rapid oxidation formed the basis of a 2009 event. *Author's collection.*

An ouroboros spectrum enticed merrymakers to participate in the 1989 spring equinox. *Author's collection.*

Left: The ninth Corn Festival took place in an unwary South Austin neighborhood. *Courtesy Tommy Bauman.*

Right: The second Corn Festival still mocked Richard Nixon's resignation. *Courtesy Tommy Bauman.*

The Uranium Savages' security arm held a birthday party in many Decembers. *Courtesy Tommy Bauman.*

The Capital City's sprightly spirit is epitomized by the Austintatious Mural on Twenty-third Street. *Public domain.*

The neighborhood salon is alive and well in Northeast Austin. *Courtesy Linda Anderson.*

Above: Bill Oliver pilots his merry and talented musicians to the far reaches of fun. *Courtesy Sam Hurt.*

Left: An allusional Super Pig wanted you to join him at the 1988 Spamarama. *Courtesy Sam Yeates.*

Independent Business Investment Zones tout the city's idiosyncratic small-scale companies. *Courtesy AIBA.*

The Honk!Tx parade begins in East Austin. *Author's collection.*

17

WILLIE NELSON'S FOURTH OF JULY PICNIC

W oodstock happened in August 1969, a pivotal event for the countercultural baby boomer generation. The notion of 400,000 people enthralled by long days and nights of music in a huge outdoor location set the pattern for other extravaganzas that followed.

In 1972, in diminutive Dripping Springs, Texas, merely thirty miles west of Austin, a group of Dallas promoters was inspired to try something similar. Calling it the Dripping Springs Reunion, it was to be almost as grand as its New York predecessor but centered on country music instead of rock 'n' roll. The staff expected 220,000 attendees, but only around 18,000 ended up coming to the Hurlbut Ranch over the course of three days. Despite the low turnout, one particular performer, whose name, Willie Nelson, was listed in tiny print at the bottom of the playbill, realized that a big rural event would be a good idea and could actually make money.

Early the next summer, almost on the spur of the moment, Willie planned his own open-air affair, booking the very same property where the reunion had been held. This was around the same time that the Cosmic Cowboy or Progressive Country music scene began to coalesce, so instead of the Nashville-type headliners of the previous year, Willie's lineup included such Texas-connected "outlaws" as Waylon Jennings, Kris Kristofferson, Rita Coolidge {What was her nickname?[53]}, John Prine and Doug Sahm. With an attendance of forty thousand, his festival was off and running as an annual thing.

The second picnic happened in College Station at Texas World Speedway, a racetrack. Locals did not invite him back. In 1975, the picnic relocated to Liberty Hill, a tiny burg just northwest of Austin. If you had been there that Friday, the first thing you'd have noticed would have been the traffic: lines of cars turning off Texas Highway 29 and Ranch Road 1869 into a big field where hundreds of other vehicles were already parked. After shutting off your engine, you'd shoulder your equipment and supplies, such as a folding lawn chair, a small ice chest with beverages and food, a water jug, your camera (no mobile phones yet), a wide-brimmed hat and, of course, your admission ticket if you procured it ahead of time for $5.50. After hiking across the parking area, you followed a trail of sorts that ran along the road, into a gate and down a slope to where the action was. You'd first behold the large, elevated stage with its canvas roof billowing in the summer breeze. Off to one side were concessions for beer or meals, and the scant toilet facilities were lined up nearby. The area in front of the stage was open, but a line of trees some distance back indicated the South Fork of the San Gabriel River, a tributary to the mighty Brazos.

Some few minutes after noon, Willie began the show, as he always does, with a lively rendition of "Whiskey River." He might have played one or two other songs, but then he stepped aside to let the other names on the program perform: Kris Kristofferson, Rita Coolidge, the Pointer Sisters, Charlie Daniels Band, Doug Sahm Quintet, Billy Swan, Alex Harvey, Johnny Bush, Donnie Fritts, Billy "C," Milton Carroll and Delbert McClinton.

You would have heard such songs as "I've Got to Have You," "Loving Arms," "Fairytale," "Betcha Got a Chick," "The South's Gonna Do It (Again)," "Long-Haired Country Boy," "Nuevo Laredo," "Groover's Paradise," "I Can Help," "There Stands the Glass," "You're Gonna Love Yourself in the Morning," "'B' Movie Boxcar Blues" and "Two More Bottles of Wine."

As always in the middle of a Texas summer, heat is an issue. Wise listeners have brought something for shade, a parasol or tarp or whatever—anything that doesn't interfere with the view of the guys behind them. Just like at Woodstock, a cloudburst does happen, and people scramble to take shelter, although the wet seems a relief from the swelter. Music stops, and the amps and other equipment get covered. The humidity after the rain becomes yet another challenge to comfort.

The canvas awning over the stage has filled with quite a bit of rainwater. It slowly leaks through the cloth, creating a steady dribble that prevents

As his popularity continued to soar, Willie Nelson and others performed in Waterloo Park in downtown Austin. *Courtesy Pauline Jacobson.*

the concert from resuming. One of the performers, a cowboy-looking fellow, walks out under the drip. Unholstering a pistol from his belt, he shoots one bullet up though the canvas. The dribble turns to a torrent. In a couple minutes, all the water has drained. The crowd erupts in its approval, crews mop up the residue and uncover the sound system and the music begins anew.

The river flows a couple hundred yards behind the audience, so you stroll down that way to check out the scene. The old Texas tradition of skinny-dipping is alive and well with these mostly young concertgoers. What better way to stay cool and relax in the company of fun-loving folks! As the afternoon wanes and the evening wears on, you hear top-notch performances by the soulful Pointer Sisters but miss the way-out wailing of otherwise-perpetual Willie buddy Leon Russell.

Promoters expected only five thousand to attend and actually planned on twenty-five thousand showing up. No one could believe it when ninety thousand ultimately came through the gates. Needless to say, sanitation facilities and security personnel were completely overwhelmed, resulting in Willie paying a $1,000 fine for violating the Texas Mass Gatherings Act.

Nelson went on to host picnics in many other locations inside and out of Texas, but he also did one in miniature in Waterloo Park in Austin in 1978. Named for the collection of log cabins that became the city of Austin, the park was created in the early 1970s by stringing together a line of former house lots into a public space along Waller Creek directly east of the capitol building. For just five dollars, you could attend either night, Saturday or Sunday, April 8 or 9. Accompanying the "family" of music makers were a street dance and craft show. The shindig's proceeds benefited the Austin Symphony, which had recently completed renovating the nearby triangular-shaped Hamilton Building as its headquarters. It anchors Symphony Square and includes an amphitheater and a couple restaurants housed in other historical structures.

Time passes, and the next time you dare to go to Willie's is in 1990, when the picnic occurs in Zilker Park with merely fifteen thousand of your closest friends. Because of the notorious inconvenience and outright danger at his other picnics, this time the situation is much more controlled. A perimeter fence surrounds the section of the park that holds the action, and strict control is imposed on people as they enter. You're allowed to bring in no more than two sealed bottles of drinking water, and you're also frisked for weapons as if you're a criminal. After that, though, you can relax and take in the great music. Headlining are the Highwaymen, who are Nelson, Waylon Jennings, Kris Kristofferson and Johnny Cash. Also on the bill is Little Joe y La Familia, which adds intercultural spice to the mix. Your favorite song that night, of course, is "The Highwayman." Not many country/western ideas relate to reincarnation, except, perhaps, rein*tar*nation, which posits coming back as a hillbilly.

And Willie keeps us picnicking.

PART III

SEASONAL SHINDIGS

18

Uranium Savages

I f you look closely at many posters advertising Austin music events, you might begin to notice the repetition of a certain numeral: 709. What in the world is this, and why does it seem to be everywhere?

To answer the riddle, you need to transport yourself backward in time some four decades. Those were heady days in this creative town. The Armadillo World Headquarters was going strong, attracting musical acts of all stripes and putting Austin on its path to branding itself the Live Music Capital. Other nightclubs, such as Soap Creek Saloon, the Split Rail and the Alliance Wagon Yard did brisk business, as well, taking full advantage of the new genre of music developing here. Legend has it that one night in the early months of the Dillo's existence, two radically diverse types of people, hippies and rednecks, were together listening to the same band and enjoying what they heard. Two such fellows, a long-hair and a goat-roper, each representing his own lifestyle, stood side by side and eyed the other with suspicion. But, hell, this is Texas, the friendly state—why not share? The hippie handed his joint to the cowboy, the cowboy offered the freak his beer and something changed. Two cultures instantly transformed into something new. Progressive Country was the next big thing, a melding of folksy rock with country-western delivered in a particular Texas accent, with Austin at its heart.

Musicians flocked to Austin and formed bands. One such bunch was a gang of surfers who had played together in southwest Houston as the Uranium Clods and the Gypsy Savages. In Austin, they appeared as the Sons of the Uranium Savage, which name they soon shortened to the Uranium Savages. Since some of the band members lived in or near Succotash Central (Palaces of Corn and Bean), that was where they made their debut.

From this association of untamed teenagers came the apocryphal tale of one particular member who, during an especially dreamy state of mind, looked up into the sky and saw the figure 709 spread over a cloud formation. The band adopted this number and made it one of its cryptic in-jokes, along with its fictitious mascot, Eddy Savage, and the motto, "Trust Us." The meaning? Zen, god, everything and nothing. Like in a secret society, those who say don't know, and those who know don't say. July 9 (for the combination of 7-0-9) they dubbed International Eddy Day, the most high holy of all days. Eddy Savage is the guru and spiritual leader. The Shrovinovers are the band's security arm. They first called themselves Shriners and wore red fezzes with scimitars until they learned that it's illegal in Texas to impersonate a Mason, even in parody. Drawing again from their youthful experience, they translated Shriner into Ovenglovish by putting the syllable *ov* in front of every pronounced vowel.

The Savages' reputation grew not because of superior musicianship but because of the sheer fun they generated in the audience, who, consequently, bought more alcoholic drinks. People went bonkers.

More than one hundred musicians have rotated in and out of the band in the past four decades, but the core cadre remains. Artly Snuff got to Austin in 1961, thanks to his military dad's retirement here. He heads the Shrovinovers who entertain the band while the band entertains the audience. Kerry Awn was among the southwest Houstonians who migrated to UT in 1970. He served as a political cartoonist for the *Daily Texan*, and he's both the lead singer in the band and its damn good poster artist. Kerry also has done stand-up comedy these many years in Austin, including seventeen of them at Esther's Follies. Other early sketchy associates included Tom "Tommy B" Bauman and Rick Turner. Those three created the Stephen F. Austin {What was his middle name?[54]} postcard mural on Twenty-third Street, which also turned forty in 2014, when it enjoyed an extensive restoration. Theresa lived in the Bean Palace next to the Corn Palace and later married Artly.

Here continues the conversation among those jovial folks at Maria's:

Artly: We've been doing celebrations for, it seems like, forty years. We're a show band. We wear costumes and do characters on stage. We tailor to anniversaries and events.

Before learning of the illegality of their name, celebrants at this rave called themselves Shriners. *Courtesy Tommy Bauman.*

Kerry: Every gig was an "event." We brought the party. We were the cocaine cowboys, the crazy hippie band.

Theresa: If you pay attention, you start seeing 709 everywhere. $7.09 is a price at the GM Steakhouse in the movie Slacker. *At Texicalli Grill* [an extinct South Austin eatery], *sandwiches were specially priced to total $7.09 when you add tax.*

Kerry: Regarding a memorable Savage appearance one year, we used to play the Ritz Theater. [Before] *the Ritz had been taken over by Jim Franklin of the Armadillo, it had been a porno theater. He fixed it up, and we got a gig there. We were playing there one Halloween* [1982], *and Sixth Street was starting to catch on then and a lot of people were there. It wasn't like it is now, of course. We were playing when someone set off a military smoke grenade just outside the building. Smoke started pouring in. Next thing you know, "Fire in a theater!" is yelled out. The fire station is only one block away on Fifth. The firefighters couldn't get to the Ritz with their trucks because there were too many people in the street. They had to form a line running into the Ritz Theater because there was a fire on Halloween with hundreds of people inside. Disaster! After they got in, they realized it wasn't a fire; it was a smoke bomb. And they got pissed, as I recall. They weren't too happy with the whole situation. The next year was when the police erected barricades and made people walk in a circle, around and around, one way. That, we thought, was our legacy, but of course, that era's gone.*

On Tuesdays, US played the One Knite. Now, that's a club that assuredly threw some parties after hours.

19

South Austin Popular Culture Center

Along with Austin's vibrant live-music scene, a complementary art form arose with it. Beginning in the Vulcan Gas Company era (1968 through 1969) and mimicking the countercultural rock concerts in San Francisco, every musical event was publicized by a poster with original artwork. These eleven- by seventeen-inch placards hung on trees at the University of Texas, power poles and building sides throughout the city. A cadre of artists, including Micael Priest, Guy Juke and Gilbert Shelton, became deft at creating the notices, usually with basic pen-and-ink methods. The posters became collectors' items in and of themselves.

Serious compilation of this type of art in this music city had begun during the heyday of the Armadillo World Headquarters, that only-in-Austin quintessential music hall. Henry Gonzalez, a fine artist himself, worked at the Dillo in the early '70s and served as its first official archivist. He carefully saved, conserved and catalogued all manner of posters, handbills, photographs and ephemera.

As the decades rolled by, art aficionados and creators realized the need for a central repository to house and display this highly specialized genre. Thus, in 2004 was born a community art collective known as the South Austin Museum of Popular Culture, which morphed into the South Austin Popular Culture Center, or SouthPop for short. It's located at 1516B South Lamar adjacent to Planet K, a "family" gift shop for folks who enjoy incense, scented candles, underground comix, indoor grow lights and alternative knickknacks. Henry's files became SouthPop's core collection. He's now its facility manager.

Curious admirers of the deft artistry of Micael Priest (right) hear his amazing tales. *Author's collection.*

Henry's partner is Leea Mechling, also a former Dillo employee. She's the center's executive director. The doors are open sporadically, "by appointment or by chance," as the phone greeting states. Six to eight times a year, SouthPop erects a new exhibit. Each show begins and ends with an opening or closing—invariably starting at 7:09 p.m.—that features artists, snacks, beer, wine, extra displays, conversation and (what else but) live music. The stage backdrop, rendered by Kerry Awn, amounts to a cartoon history of all things Austin. {Who's the fellow riding the chariot?[55]}

In addition to the center's shop, which sells prints, postcards and signs, outside is another permanent display, the Memorial Wall, which is dedicated to the dearly departed Austinites and Texans who made our lives worth living.

One artist, Nels "Jagmo" Jacobson, puts it this way:

> *In Austin, Texas, particularly, poster art provides a formidable counterpoint to a thriving live music tradition. Austin posters and popular music are each manifestations of the same maverick urge—to buck the system and to define reality on one's own terms. And in the same way that rock & roll itself is a progressive, persistent defiance of the status quo, from the days of the Vulcan to the Dillo, and then Raul's, and…the Black Cat, the poster art of*

Shiva's Headband, a longtime Austin original, rocks the South Austin Popular Culture Center during a poster exhibit event. *Author's collection.*

Greenery, flowers and mementos adorn frames at SouthPop. *Author's collection.*

each succeeding generation has consumed its progenitors. As such, Austin's poster tradition is reborn in the rambunctious vision of every new guitar slinger or renegade garage band. For postering in Austin is largely an act of creative solidarity and a labor of love, and as long as live music flourishes, uncompromising and original, so too will the poster art that celebrates it.[56]

20

FULL MOON BARN DANCE

Leeann Atherton first came to Austin in 1987 from Charleston, South Carolina, by way of Nashville, Tennessee. She had heard tell of Austin's tuneful scene, and after a brief visit, she settled her affairs up north and then came to stay in 1988. Leeann almost immediately fell in with Willie Nelson, Robert Earl Keen and Rich Brotherton. The latter produced her first album, which blended blues, folk, Americana and gospel. Typical of independent musicians, Leeann released the album on her own label and continued to seek venues in which to sell CDs and perform her songs. She wanted, however, something better than a bar.

She didn't have far to look. In 1990, two doors away from where she was renting in South Austin, Leeann found a dwelling for sale—a house on a large corner lot—that conveniently included an aging, wooden three-car garage. With its bare weathered walls and corrugated metal roof, the thing looked like a barn. Behind it, the lot sloped down to a corner and then extended away from the street, along the rear of the stone house, and past a free-standing apartment. Scattered juniper and oak trees gave shade. Even though surrounded by suburbia, this haven retained a rural feel. She bought it.

In Leeann grew a burning desire to create not just a setting for her own music but also a place to give back to the community of which she was a part. Back in Nashville, she'd associated with the New Grass Revival and had sat in with their Full Moon Pickin' Parties, which remain laid-back, family-friendly events that feature Middle Tennessee's finest bluegrass music under the light of a full moon. That seemed like paradise to her, but she'd left it behind to discover another musical paradise in central Texas. This one had Barton Springs, great rivers, marvelous music makers and right-on radio. She transplanted the pickin' notion to South Austin in her just-acquired property.

Initially, recitals happened inside the barn, with fiddler Erik Hokannen the first to occupy the spotlight. But audiences quickly outgrew the space. Over time, Leeann built a stage (also with a metal roof) in the lot's corner and added a painted plywood dance floor. This became the center for her frequent jam sessions and dance concerts on the Sunday closest to the full moon at least four times a year. The early sessions featured food contests to determine who could create the best potluck meal. A notable winner was a woman from Hawaii who brought Lotta Inches Enchiladas. A hand-painted sign dubbed the barn Little Luckenbach. To raise money for the burgeoning events, Leeann and fellow singer Toni Price sold homemade buttons, suitable for evening wear, on which a cow jumped over the moon.

Even when not near a lunar brilliance, the barn also saw weddings, jubilee dinners, Easter egg hunts, Christmas nights, Halloween shows and fundraising events for nonprofits like SOS and Camp Casey. Things truly expanded when Leeann connected her venue with South by Southwest (SXSW), the Capital City's huge music and media explosion that comes around every year for a week in March. She made a point of booking great

The spacious yard at the Full Moon Barn Dance accommodates plenty of music aficionados. *Author's collection.*

From Leeann Atherton's stage comes a variety of words and tunes. *Author's collection.*

but unsigned local bands. As the crowds swelled, she hired extra personnel such as a doorkeeper and sound engineer. Leeann's Sunday evening showcase at SXSW features composers and performers from all over the country and Europe. Several, such as the Real Ones of Norway, the Hedvig Mollestad Trio, Sweden's Baskery, Burton and the FreeFallers and Peter Rowan (writer of "Panama Red"), make the Barn Dance their favored recurring venue. Other touring soloists arrive from Germany, Japan and France.

When you attend, you carry a covered dish to share and contribute with an admission donation. Food and snacks get laid out on a couple of big tables. Beer flows from a keg, and iced bottles fill a banged-up canoe. Rows of ramshackle wooden benches and tables offer seating in front of the barn and alongside it. Two powerful public-address speakers hang from the stage rafters and a nearby tree. The control booth sits beneath an extension of the barn. The sound system amply (pun intended) fills the space with booming music.

Leeann Atherton's Full Moon Barn Dance occurs several times each year. This group gathers during South by Southwest. *Author's collection.*

Likely the loudest service on a Sunday morning in Austin, Hippie Church could be confused with a concert. *Author's collection.*

Bands and soloists stand on colorful carpets in front of decorative bedspread curtains on which hangs a symbolic blue Planet Austin. You can hang out the barn's windows, enjoying excellent views of the stage and dance floor. Inside the barn are vintage Leeann gig posters and other examples of hippie art. Two portable toilets provide relief. Professional and volunteer cooks attend a covered barbecue grill, and a campfire next to the house creates a focus for acoustic music after the amplified show ends. Often crafts people set up their wares for sale or demonstration, and strolling magicians work the crowd.

The barn brings folks closer to the earth on particularly human terms: barefoot, outdoors, with easy conversation, food, music and fun in a welcoming, open atmosphere that feels like old Austin but is still "now" Austin. You just cannot beat a song circle around a campfire or open mic where everybody's playing.[57]

Leeann prefers to perform in red cowgirl boots and loves living in a party zone. She's already home. Students at Pease Elementary School (the oldest in Austin) don't realize how lucky they are to have Leeann as their music teacher. She's also the major player at Hippie Church, which has for nearly twenty years given dancers and glad people a place to show their devotion to movement and gospel music at Maria's Taco Xpress on South Lamar, the location where she also belts it out every Friday.

21

Austin Independent Business Alliance

Another rich source of social events is the office, business or professional organization. People who work together in a company or who apply themselves to similar professions often get together to network or share ideas and common concerns. One such group that is tied specifically to Austin's unique character is the Austin Independent Business Alliance. AIBA was founded in 2001 by Carolyn Phillips of the *Austin Chronicle*, Steve Bercu of Book People and Rebecca Melançon of *The Good Life* magazine. In 2008, it absorbed another similar nonprofit, Choose Austin First. Today, its members number some four hundred.

One of the factors that makes Austin unique is the high percentage of locally owned businesses here. Officially sanctioned, assisted and encouraged by municipal government, small mom-and-pop companies stand at the forefront of the local economy. From every dollar spent at a local business, forty-five cents of it stays in the city. That's a marked contrast of the mere thirteen cents of each dollar spent at a large, national, corporate chain. The much-touted slogan "Keep Austin Weird" became a rallying cry to support local business in 2008 and was encouraged by the AIBA, the web address of which is "ibuylocal."

The organization identified clusters of small businesses in several places within the city and created an independent business investment zone, or IBIZ, in each area. Using the concept of co-marketing, the Alliance publishes brochures and flyers that list and highlight local firms in each IBIZ. South Lamar is one district that counts thirty shops and outlets, and those in Lo-Burn (lower Burnet Road) exceed fifty in number.

The alliance sponsors mixers several times a year, wherein members—which include not just retail merchants but also insurance firms, medical clinics, plumbers, tour guides, remodelers and massage therapists—get together and enjoy local food, beverages and live music while trading ideas, participating in seminars and cultivating cross-industrial collaborations. Such parties meet at a local bar, restaurant or facility such as Capital Cruises, a pleasure boat company that offers gliding rides around Lady Bird Lake. During a typical mixer, the attendees may not appear overtly

This page, top: The Austin Independent Business Alliance (AIBA) is all about local. *Courtesy AIBA.*

This page, bottom: Independent business owners enjoy local food and drink on an AIBA boat ride. *Author's collection.*

Opposite, top: The organization encourages Austinites to spend their money in town. *Courtesy AIBA.*

Opposite, bottom: Members and friends of AIBA socialize on Lady Bird Lake. *Author's collection.*

strange or eccentric, but all members share a strong desire to offer goods and services that reflect the area's unique culture. Most of the mixers are free and open to potential members.

Similarly, groups of businesses in investment zones work together to throw monthly brouhahas to attract interest to their turf. In mid-2014, East End and East Sixth began blending their celebrations on fourth Fridays. The latter sector is often called "Deep Sixth" because it's east of I-35, to distinguish it from "Dirty Sixth," Austin's most visible party central. East End is that section of Eleventh Street just east of the freeway, the traditional black downtown, where stand such revered institutions as Victory Grill and the Texas Music Museum. The two zones are only five blocks from each other, so combining their efforts creates a multiplier effect.

Mark your calendar.

22

CASA NEVERLANDIA

James Talbot came to Austin in 1977 after earning a degree in architecture and fine arts at Rice University. He broadened his awareness and skill with explorations of tapestry, jewelry making, welding, playspace design, ceramics and nonferrous metalwork sculpture at the University of Texas, Austin Community College, Dougherty Art Center and Laguna Gloria Art School. He works in all these media.

It is Talbot's living situation, however, that sets him apart from other artists. In 1979, he bought an 1,100-square-foot bungalow built in 1906 in a close-in South Austin subdivision. There, for approximately twenty years, he began a remodeling project that utterly changed the old cottage into what's likely this city's weirdest, most inventive house. Talbot calls it Casa Neverlandia.

What was once a single story now stretches into the sky as high as three. The roof is transformed from a simple gable to a soaring A-frame. Instead of wooden siding on the outside, the walls are brick inlaid with mosaic and tile of many colors, as well as native limestone rock and rounded plaster. And that's just the outside.

You might get invited to tour the casa or to attend a house concert there. Walk up the rough steps to the cozy porch and notice the array of pot lids, xylophones and bells mounted on the front screen door. Pick up a mallet made from a hardwood stick and strike up a tune on the noisemakers. A voice emanating from a PVC pipe sticking out from the doorjamb will tell you to wait a bit. Momentarily, a smallish man of indeterminate age clad in patterned chef pants, a solid-color T-shirt and sandals will appear and grant you ingress.

You're in the chamber of the Four Elements. To your left is the Earth Altar, a bricolage of geodes and rock crystals built into the wall and which, as Talbot explains, contains his father's ashes. To your right, down a step, sits the living room. Facing you against the west wall is the Rumford fireplace, which is built into a cranny and recessed below the floor. To your right is the Air Space, a bank of bay windows framed in several hues of blue to match the sky. The Water Wall rises to your left. It's a four-foot-wide mosaic made entirely of mirror fragments from which juts eyes, nose, cheeks and lips. The kitchen's out back, and Talbot's showroom and office are behind you on the house's opposite edge, but you and the other guests continue along the entry's original trajectory through a curtained portal and up a short flight of steps.

At the top of those stairs you head either left or right and find yourself in an enormous sanctuary beneath the A-frame roof. "Welcome to the Bali Room," says Talbot. If it's a tour, he points out the reed-fencing ceiling with its round red beams and bamboo outlines and the grass-mat walls that slope slightly outward from the carpeted floor. Facing the street is a raised platform over which stands an interior loft accessible by a ladder. Doors to the right lead to an exterior balcony. The whole scene gains golden illumination from a continuous ridge skylight high above, which serves double duty by venting warm air out the top.

Above the steps you came up are more stairs, these lined with a nautical rope ladder leading to another landing, where an additional flight ascends to the bedroom. Two octagonal interior windows cut through the wall, and a brass tabletop crowns the doorway, which is also framed in red. From this airy upper level, you get the feeling of being in the treetops, and Talbot tells you how much he enjoys waking up in the canopy.

If you're here for the house concert, you take a seat on one of the chairs or improvised bleachers or you lean comfortably against the sloping wall. The band is set up opposite you and soon begins to play. If it's Mad Agnes, a Connecticut trio of a man and wife and another woman, they begin what could be described as transcendent Celtic music with guitar, percussion, keyboard and sweet vocal harmonies. Their original songs cover humor, love, sorrow—the entire range of human emotion. If you had to pick a favorite number, it would be "Manic Depressive Madrigal." After their set, the group processes out, taking advantage of the casa's secret passageways and singing a cappella to make their exit. Guests

Organic shapes greet visitors in the entryway of Casa Neverlandia. *Author's collection.*

Left: James Talbot explains the natural lighting inside Casa Neverlandia's main room. *Author's collection.*

Below: The element of water is represented by a three-dimensional mosaic of mirror fragments inside Casa Neverlandia. *Author's collection.*

Opposite: The third level of Casa Neverlandia soars into the tree canopy. *Author's collection.*

relish the special popcorn and the mango lime mint punch after the show out on the back deck.

The series of events began in earnest in 1997 with a housewarming to honor the new tall roof and its dry-in. If not to hear Mad Agnes, Talbot has invited people over for chocolate tastings, Boggle games, potluck banquets, creativity classes, talent shows, poetry readings and birthday parties for himself and his then-partner, Kay. Art food dinners compelled invitees to get creative with their food: one guest brought a potato carved and garnished like a couch; someone else contributed a Jell-O sculpture. For a performance art affair, each attendee took a turn at being Ruler of the Universe. The candidate was outfitted with a scepter, diadem and raiment and sat on a throne for thirty minutes. Adoring subjects asked the potentate what he or she would do with ultimate power. How big would your dreams be? A scribe sat nearby, recording the proceedings.

Kay's birthday was all about personal empowerment for her, a wonder woman. She had never earned an actual college degree but had for many years worked for academics. In truth, she needed no officially sanctioned certificate. So, reminiscent of the Wizard of Oz, Talbot and friends bestowed on her a diploma, on which was listed all her accomplishments. They barely all fit on the paper she had so many. Prominent was an MSU (for "making stuff up").

The abode is a place of many places: Talbot figures upward of two hundred people could occupy the various cubbyholes, corners, nooks and alcoves with easy movement among them and to the outside. Social intercourse naturally flows into the backyard, where stand Talbot's several workshops and a four-story observation tower equipped with solar panels, playground ladders and a fireman's pole for quick descent. You're reminded of the lines in Willy Wonka: "What is this, a funhouse?" "Why? Having fun?"

Talbot considers his experience to be, essentially, camping, especially thanks to his hearth: primal, nurturing, alive. The installation's slow but steady construction and refinement reflect its creator's inner growth. His home is legitimately a gift to the neighborhood and a monumental encouragement for others to get creative, too. Casa Neverlandia is all about celebration, openness, flexibility and, ultimately—like so much of Austin—self-expression.[58]

Top: Brave souls cross the catwalk during a tour of Casa Neverlandia. *Author's collection.*

Bottom: Casa Neverlandia's creator and resident, James Talbot, appears relaxed in a T-shirt and patterned chef's pants. *Author's collection.*

23
AUDIORICH PRODUCTIONS

It all started on November 11, 1977, when I, your intrepid author, hosted a unique event that incorporated many elements—music, food, beverages, decor, attire and guests—around a central organizing idea. With the success of that first "Cosmo Party," never would I throw a mere "normal" function, and a long series of themed celebrations began. What followed has been an enormous outpouring of entertainments presented in public places and in a succession of residences. A website puts forth names, dates, locations, capsule descriptions and other details of the socials. Most of the parties happened only once, but several noteworthy ones bore repeating, as we'll see.

About the music: Every gathering had an associated soundtrack created for the party's specific theme. The songs were sequenced not just because of their relation to the motif but also in a sensible order. This is what expert, regularly employed disc jockeys do any time they're on the air. Those of us who work less regularly often store or "can" such a program, which could be repeatedly enjoyed. In analog days, I recorded the collections onto reel-to-reel tapes from LPs, 45s, cassettes, videotapes or other reels. At slow speed, one tape played for three hours and twelve minutes at reduced but acceptable fidelity. Each music mix required almost double the time to research, find, arrange, set up and dub. Playlists were handwritten onto yellow legal-pad paper trimmed to fit inside a seven-inch tape box. Most of the fifty-plus original reels were eventually digitized.

About the invitations: Word of each affair came in a notice that the host either gave or sent to prospective guests. The early flyers were hand drawn,

Time for celebration—a celebration of time. *Author's collection.*

then duplicated and distributed. Presenters for twenty years were Vickenhow Productions, which combined the names of my then-wife, Vicki, and mine. More recently, I also have employed computer graphics to supplement the handcraftiness. Like posters from rock concerts of old, these summons have become collectibles themselves.

What's the occasion? What's not the occasion! Along with my fascination with almanacs and calendars came a heightened awareness of solstices, equinoxes and the cross-quarter days in between. Each such earth-sky time point presented itself as a celebratory opportunity: Groundhog Day, vernal equinox, May Day, summer solstice, Lammas, autumnal equinox, Halloween and winter solstice. To the planners (myself and spouse), eight parties a year sounded reasonable and feasible in addition to the usual birthdays and anniversaries. Most of those fell on other, not-so-cosmic dates. The astronomical "holidays," however, suggested themes in and of themselves, many of which gelled into events that became annual and regular.

Stellar Positronic Astro-Celestial Entertainment (SPACE), inaugurated in 1979, came around several times. It drew energy from the enormous popularity of *Star Wars* and played on nostalgia lingering from *Star Trek*. Those two features supplied most of the party's soundtrack, along with a generous dose of Gustav Holst's "The Planets." Guests were admonished to don helmets and carry blasters. Because of its connection to the U.S. space program, Tang was the beverage of choice, spiked with rocket fuel.

In contrast to going into outer galactic realms, the Cool Jazz and Blue Cave event headed underground in 1979. Reflecting my newfound appreciation of the jazz genre, I showcased such artists as Stanley Clark, Chick Corea and Oscar Peterson. I then presented a slide show of nearby Texas commercial caverns like Inner Space and Natural Bridge

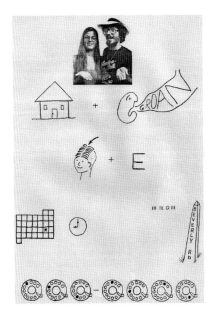

If you couldn't solve the puzzle, you weren't invited. *Author's collection.*

while tracking the recently released *Journey to the Centre of the Earth* album by Rick Wakeman.

Growing up under the influence of our engineer dad, my childhood family boasted much pioneering technology in small suburban Corpus Christi in the early '60s. We had the first stereo on the block and the first tape recorder, a Heathkit. I was totally into sound and often invited school friends over to make silly music and spoken-word recordings. I continued that interest and activity into college, choosing to study radio, television and film. By the early '80s, I'd amassed such an impressive collection of homegrown programs that they became the theme of a party and its soundtrack. Its invitation was a rebus: little pictures drawn to represent words or parts of words. A product of its time, the phone number was depicted as a series of seven rotary-dial images with the pertinent numeral finger hole filled in.

The summer solstice also provided much material for more whoop-de-doos. The longest day of the year practically begs for a protracted event and one that heeds the heat. It's especially important to set up a vertical shaft outside at local noon to see the shortest shadow of the year cast onto the ground. Themes for these parties included shade, fire, sun and sweaty dancing, and at least a couple invitations announced the affair in staggering alliteration.

Of all the celebrations, one of the most esteemed was the '60s Marathon, the first of which ran on March 10, 1979. A main characteristic was its astounding epic length: nine hours to begin with and then expanding to twelve, fourteen and thirty-eight hours, often filling an entire weekend, day and night. The other hallmark was presenting the pop and rock hit songs in chronological order. It was as if a radio signal had returned to Earth after a trip to the far reaches of the universe, faithfully replaying all songs from the decade. Folks of the baby boomer generation were able to relive their youth and formative years. Besides dressing in such obvious attire as miniskirts, bell-bottoms and beads, revelers delighted in such period activities as Volkswagen van painting, graffiti wall scrawling and uninhibited gyrating. Floor pallets and crash pads were provided for die-hard participants.

The '60s Marathon found its biggest audience when I offered it as my class project during Jerry Dean's History of Rock 'n' Roll class at the University of Texas in 1980. All five hundred students in the course were invited. The party took place on a November Friday in the Student Union Ballroom on campus, beginning at 3:00 p.m. and continuing until the wee hours. Participants brought snacks and soft drinks, and the Union sold beer to of-age attendees. I set up

The 1960s came back to UT in 1980 with much fanfare. *Author's collection.*

three huge blank white boards for the graffiti wall, and a bank of black-light posters occupied another corner. In the tradition of that colorful decade, we also presented a light show. An overhead projector held two nesting clear-glass pie plates. A mixture of pale yellow cooking oil and dyed water went into the outer plate. When the second plate was placed into the first, the image cast upon the screen swirled and blobbed to the beat of the music. Psychedelic, man! I earned an A.

Relationships developed that fateful night: Professor Jerry Dean met Pat Griggasy, who was not in the class but had spontaneously wandered into the ballroom, drawn by the groovy tunes. They married a year later—to the day—at my family's ranch south of Austin.

Miscellaneous these and those included a beatnik coffeehouse with live poetry, berets and finger snapping; Imbolg, the Celtic name for Groundhog Day, was a celebration of marriage; Old New Year Gala on the vernal equinox is when most ancient calendars began; comedy, which we held on funny dates such as August 8, 1980 (8-8-80) and August 8, 1988 (8-8-88), offered jokes and jests; the Flower Shower praised springtime blooms; Quetzalcoatl Equinox honored snakes and rainbows; Baggins' Birthday

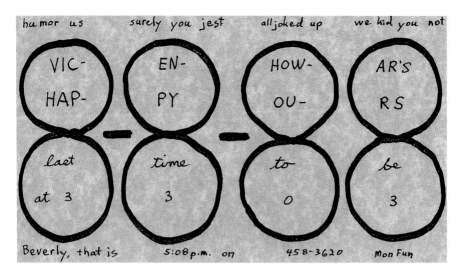

What were you doing on the eighth day of the eighth month of the eighty-eighth year? Now, that's funny! *Author's collection.*

Bash, which invitation was printed inside a gold ring, recalled our favorite hobbit uncle-and-nephew team.

The Revived Unbirthday Party in 1991 was a memorial to Steven Stepan, the artist of the UT '60s Marathon invitation and an overall fascinating character, who always threw this on his own birthday, February 16; the Equine Equinox honored horses and their riders; my fortieth birthday in 1982 took notice of time, as opposed to space; Night and Day, held on the vernal equinox of '93, featured equal doses of songs, half about the day and half about the night.

We held a Train Dance (trained aunts?) in recognition of locomotives; a Prehistoric Primavera faced fossil fascination, which fueled a riotous reptilian romp; the Grass Blast happened in gratitude for prairies; since spring is the season of wind, we could do none other than a Bean Break (fun with flatulent foods) or to put on A Certain Air party; several events toasted my hometown of Corpus Christi and my classmates who also moved to Austin, collectively known as the Capital Corpuscle Coterie; since an equinox offers the mirror image of light and dark, our trip to Wonderland through the looking glass included hedgehog croquet, a mad tea party, a general unbirthday observance and a hookah; and in the year '07, we noted my fifth-and-a-half decade by Goin' 55 with an evening of car songs.

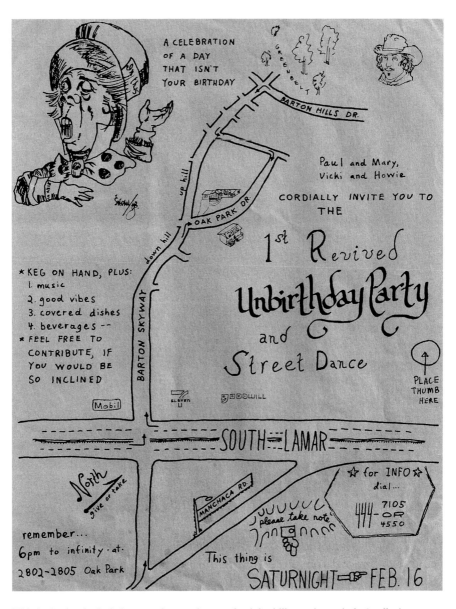

This invitation included a map, instructions and original illustrations. *Author's collection.*

Equal parts noon and midnight informed this springtime theme. *Author's collection.*

One particular structure that greatly boosted congeniality at the South Austin dwelling was the yurt. Modeled after a Mongolian tent, the muffin-shaped plywood hut sat in the side yard within easy access of the home's back door. A group of twenty volunteers erected the yurt in just four days in the autumn of 1994. Its inventor and the project coordinator was William S. Coperthwaite, a curious and clever scholar of social design. Hanging out in the yurt was plenty of fun because its roundness and comfortably sloped walls enhanced conversation. The acoustics seemed to amplify voices and guitars. You felt sheltered but not confined. One central candle lit the whole space, and smoldering sticks of incense kept mosquitoes at bay. Visitors to the yurt in the yard found it ideal for the three Ms: music, meditation and merriment.

Two oft-repeated themes proved to be best loved. The first Jungle Junket came about in 1992, a fab rain forest fest for nearly one hundred folks, an attendance record. Almost as regular has been the Ocean Scene, a shiver-me-timbers saltwater celebration. Certain movie nights henceforth occur on pertinent dates each year: *Black Orpheus* on Mardi Gras, *The Alamo* on March

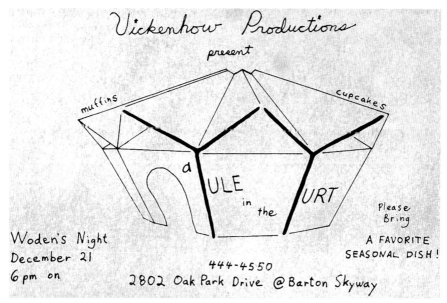

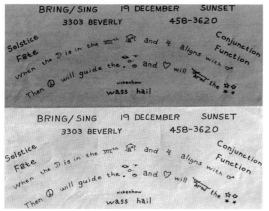

Above: The *Y*s are implied in the design. *Author's collection.*

Left: The Conjunction Function corresponded with the 1986 winter solstice. *Author's collection.*

6, *The Wicker Man* on May Day, *Midsummer Night's Dream* on June 21 and *V for Vendetta* on the fifth of November.

The biggest, most elaborate and longest running of all blowouts revolves around the winter solstice. Discovering that the modern traditions of Christmas had much older heathen roots, we hosts sought to re-create and expand on those original meanings. The longest, darkest night on the calendar easily necessitates luminous compensation in the form of candles, lanterns and hearth fires. Add the pragmatic notion of feasting to prepare for the lean, cold season, and the party is already created. The series officially commenced in 1981 and hasn't missed a year since.

More than just a get-together around a central idea, this fête involves a staged performance, reusable songbooks and audience participation. Drawing freely from an amalgamation of northern European traditions, the winter solstice must be held indoors and set before a fireplace, bringing the primeval bonfire inside. Evergreen foliage is present, as are sparkly decorations and tonsorial finery. There's usually a theme within the theme, as well—trees, astral conjunction, Roman Saturnalia, snowflakes, mistletoe, tapers, angels, ancestors, children, beasts, green men, elves or fools multiply the delight. At least two yules were in celebration of the yurt.

Then came the Green Man.

Residing on the free-spirited Upper East Side of Austin offers many amenities, but our friends and neighbors there bemoaned the paucity of a place to hang out and just talk. Like in other aging suburban subdivisions, ours offers no convenient gathering point within easy walking distance. That, and usually bars are way too noisy and coffee shops way too quiet. Where would the tradition of Les Amis resume? Where could we get together, hear one another without strain and foment revolution?

In the summer of 2009, wife Linda was off from her art teaching job and dabbling in various projects. One was painting what she called "wish shingles," which were signs for people who wanted to change professions or start a business. When you hang out your shingle, your company is real from then on. Blending that notion with our quest for community, she executed a British pub–style sign emblazoned as the Green Man Coffee House.

The namesake deserves a backstory. Before we met in 2003, Linda traveled to England to research green men as part of her fascination with legends, fairy tales and folk figures. The Green Man is an ancient fertility symbol that can still be seen in the uppermost parts of old cathedrals and churches. When England turned from Catholic to Anglican, most of the old saintly symbols were destroyed—but not the Green Man. Typically, he's a woodland creature with vines and branches growing out of his mouth and ears. The guardian of the forest, he keeps a patient and watchful eye on all living things, ensuring their preservation and growth. I, too, had heard of Jack in the Green and other similar personages in my study of pre-Christian European religions. This knowledge was something Linda and I held in common and a big reason for our mutual attraction. Thus, it was a no-brainer to name our co-creative outlet for him.

At first we envisioned a movable feast: wherever the sign hung was to be the coffeehouse. But we had just added a spacious, covered front porch to our modest dwelling, and it immediately suggested itself as the Green

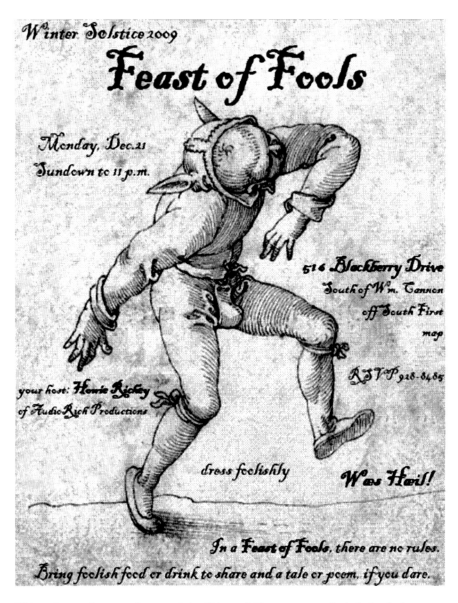

This cockamamie carousal crowned the Abbess of Unreason, as well. *Author's collection.*

Above: Conversationalists of all ages and viewpoints find interesting connections at the Green Man Coffee House. *Author's collection.*

Left: The Green Man's "shrine sign" tells neighbors that the coffeehouse is open. *Author's collection.*

Man. We arranged random chairs and benches in a circle and installed a chimenea, awnings and a bar and *poof*: we had a coffeehouse, albeit an informal, occasional one. As proprietors, we deemed to "open" the facility every Friday evening. Neighbors and friends came with potluck offerings of snacks and beverages. In addition to opportunities for the close conversation we craved, we also began to assign a theme to each episode. These we gleaned from anything notable in the almanac for that particular day: anniversaries, birthdays, death days or historical happenings. The evening's theme encouraged costumes and included germane music, decorations, libations and cuisine.

Many of the subjects and playlists of past gatherings are recycled and repurposed for the Green Man. About once a month, we present live soloists or small bands on the front porch and, since May 2011, in a theater in the backyard. We hear poets and storytellers and politicians and comedians, and we show slides and films. We publish a blog, maintain a web page and mail out weekly invitations to a select group of insiders. For them, the Green Man is the place to be every Friday that remains.

PART IV

MONTHLY AFFAIRS

24

SNAKE ISLAND

At the east end of Lady Bird Lake, in the middle of its widest extent, stands a triangular piece of land. Barely an acre in size and considered part of Austin's city park system, the isolated clump of trees was officially named Habitat Island late in 2013. In season, white herons and other waterfowl roost there. For a group of urban pirates, however, the place has long been known as Snake Island, presumably to repel tourists and other snoopers. For a number of years, Snake Island has been the scene of a succession of gatherings on the nights of full moons. The questionable legitimacy of using the property for such get-togethers casts an outlaw glamour on the event.

In 1991, the Lower Colorado River Authority (LCRA), a quasi-governmental agency in charge of a series of water impoundments along the Texas Colorado River, responded to growing environmental sentiment by creating the Colorado River Trail. In its mission statement for this initiative, the LCRA acknowledged that central Texans had for too long turned their backs on this longest of Texas's streams. To draw more attention to water quality and to help people explore the river, the authority promoted a wide variety of activities and programs, such as canoe trips, festivals, banquets, historical presentations and other fun. In the tradition of musical flotillas down the Grand Canyon on that other Colorado River, which featured singer-songwriters, the LCRA contracted local Austin soloists and guitar players to paddle along on trips and entertain participants with water-related ballads and ecologically focused lyrics.

One such musician was William "Bill" Oliver, long known in Austin as Mr. Habitat for his green ditties like "Barton Springs Eternal," "Friend of the River" and "Turtle Island." He also calls himself Captain Bilgewater, especially when wearing a distinctive yacht skipper hat and carrying Noodles, his five-foot overstuffed catfish. Outfitting companies furnished canoes, kayaks, rafts and transport logistics. One such supplier was Joe Kendall, founder of Camp Chautauqua and later director of the Texas River School, a provider of educational river trips to schoolchildren. When these two gentlemen got together, an amazing synergy ensued. River runs grew more elaborate.

Bill needed more space and flexibility than a typical canoe or kayak could provide. He teamed up with a different Joe, "Glitter" Joe Riddell, a retired lawyer who fancies handmade sparkly garments in which he gambols with abandon. Together this pair invented a raft built of plywood sheets lashed to a couple canoes. They named it the Huck Finn/Mark Twain series, one of which sported not only a hut on top but also a wood-burning stove. The zany contraption was part of many festive floats downriver, usually adjacent to other watercraft with folks who appreciated the music.

Finding a two-canoe surface too small for dances, Bill and Glitter soon expanded to three canoes with plywood measuring twelve by sixteen feet. Christened *Lady of the Lake*, the larger boat found permanent mooring in Lady Bird Lake and took part in dozens of river parades, bat-watching floats and concert listen-ins. The current workhorse of Snake Island events, it's silently propelled by a tiny electric trolling motor powered by two rechargeable twelve-volt batteries. A wooden bench is built onto the stem, under which are piled the requisite number of life vests. In case of technological failure, paddles are at hand as a backup.

The pirates who host Snake Island happenings, primarily Glitter Joe and Captain Bilgewater, decide when the full moon parties go on. Glitter's well-worded e-mail invitations provide detailed information and set the mood:

THE KREWE OF THE MYSTIC MOONLIGHT invites you and kindred spirits to join us for a Potluck/BYOB celebration of Fat Tuesday on Snake Island, near Longhorn Dam at the east end of Lady Bird Lake. Dress up and bring something to share for this special evening, March 4th.

The Krewe will offer ferry rides to and from Snake Island aboard the renowned Lady of the Lake *raft every hour on the hour from 5 PM to 11 PM. The ferry will depart from the dock on the south shore of the lake near the Austin Hostel, 2200 South Lakeshore Boulevard. Park your* *vehicles in the lot or on the street. Do not park on the grass (potential $30 ticket). Return ferries will continue until the island is cleared. Mardi Gras is over at midnight. Anyone on the island after that will be part of the clean-up crew.*

LOGISTICS
The Krewe will provide basic drinks, utensils, food, and music. Chef JR is cooking up some gumbos (seafood and veggie versions), red beans (meat and veggie versions), and rice. Please bring something to share—tasty food, your favorite beverage, a musical instrument, a log for the fire, or beads or some other Mardi Gras treat. Also, bring some cash since we will be taking donations for the Health Alliance for Austin Musicians (HAAM). We'll have face paints and some beads. Purple, gold, and green clothing is encouraged. Dress warmly but wildly. A cold evening is forecast. We'll have some campfires. You can stay warm dancing and singing. Please bring no kids or dogs, because they scare the snakes. Bring a drinking vessel and even a plate if you can. If you want a comfortable seat, bring a folding chair. This is a spirited do-it-ourselves celebration, indulging before Lent.

Usually, a couple of full vans bring the night's equipment to the dock, where helpers load the stuff onto the *Lady*. Besides tables, chairs, stoves, ice chests and a bucket toilet, the merry crew brings kerosene torches, strings of electric lights, utensils, bowls, plates, recycling and trash containers, firewood and a hand truck. The quiet cruise takes about ten minutes, depending on wind, and the raft makes landfall at the island's east cove. With flat nylon straps, hands tie the craft to exposed roots, unload and tote the cargo to the central fire area. In no time, Glitter's kitchen is up and running, basic decorations hang from trees, cloths are spread over tables, the fire begins to smolder and snacks and beverages get laid out.

The *Lady*'s official capacity is eight persons. Various pirates take turns piloting the ferry runs, picking up and dropping off revelers at either the hostel dock or the closer Point, the end of a narrow peninsula closer to the island. The voyage is half the fun, with passengers telling jokes or singing songs. Once or twice the boat capsized due to improper loading or distraction, but no serious injuries were reported.

Always represented by excellent Austin musicians, the circle around the campfire is filled with sing-along tunes and kinetic dancers. Besides the expected guitars, artists might also bring a dobro, saxophone, fiddle, percussion, flute or horn. The party's theme helps determine what songs are performed. For instance, on Fat Tuesday, revelers enjoyed Cajun- and New Orleans–style pieces such as "Jambalaya," "Mardi Gras Mambo" and "Crescent City."

One night, after years of carefree, unmolested adventures, the police came calling. Their duty was to remind the partygoers that the isle was city parkland and thus subject to all standard rules of use: no overnight camping, no defacing and a midnight curfew. After that, the gatherings didn't go long into the early morning hours as in the past, but they remain exciting and fun in their brevity. Just like observant low-impact campers, the pirates take nothing but photographs and leave nothing but footprints.

In late 2013, City of Austin planning documents recommended banning humans from Habitat Island. We're keeping a patched eye on developments.

25

The Perpetual Potluck Picnic, aka Jim O's

Eagerly anticipated every month, the Triple P is spearheaded by locally renowned natural foods caterer Jim O'Brien. This tall, muscular, sky-blue-eyed Paul Newman lookalike, film crew feeder and outdoor folk fest vendor arrived in Texas from Michigan in 1981, part of a wave of such immigrants who came out of the aging Midwest Rust Belt. His first goal was to attend school, but after a couple semesters at Sam Houston State University in Huntsville, Jim O' had second thoughts.

> *I didn't take well to college. Eventually I pulled out of there, and Austin was within reach, financially and otherwise. So I just came here and started looking around. [I] worked in a couple of restaurants, waiter jobs, for five years and evolved. I learned food service by showing up at the East West Center, a new-ager, macrobiotic, kinda cooler-than-thou white folks. So I volunteered all the time because I was in a period when I didn't have a job and I didn't have anything to do, so I went there and volunteered all the time, just 'cuz it was cool. That's how I started dabbling with big, shiny stainless steel pots. I was like, ah—I can do this. And the rest is history.*[59]

Soon Jim O' became recognized for his tasty meals at environmental organizations' camp outs.

Jim O' found an inexpensive place for rent in South Austin on Melridge Street early in 1987. To commemorate the move, he invited friends over for dinner. "What can I bring?" Unlike at many fancy, catered parties, guests to this one were encouraged to bring a covered dish with enough to share. Initially, only vegetarian items were on the serving table. And hardly anyone brought beer. That would change.

The first potluck was such a success that Jim O' deemed to repeat it a week later and then again in another week. After a short time, it became monthly. Needing a better space, Jim O' fixed up the small backyard and equipped it with chairs, benches, picnic tables, serving surfaces, ice chests, faucets, sinks, folk and found art, kerosene torches, oil lanterns, directional and informational signs that point "That-a-Way," a fountain, a performance stage, trash and recycling receptacles, colorful lighting and—importantly—a fire pit.

Fitting for the Live Music Capital, music always brings people together in Austin, and nothing helps this more than a flame. The best party sites in the city feature an open fireplace surrounded by chairs. String players and vocalists provide tunes and opportunities to join the singing, but quiet conversation remains the most effective cohesion-building activity.

The event developed through years of experience, and guests came to expect certain consistent treatment. As a caterer, Jim O' is especially renowned for his hot chai, a kind of black tea blended with herbs and spices, such as cardamom and ginger. It's especially tasty with a scoop of ice cream added. He always serves chai plus one or two "starter" dishes such as beans and rice. The aroma of his cooking seems to penetrate the whole property and everything on it. And because he's a caterer, the serving tables come fully equipped with plates, bowls, utensils, napkins, towels, trays, warmers, tongs, spatulas and spoons. Beer and wine flow abundantly, but this isn't a place for drunks.

Other additions to the backyard made guests feel welcome. A small hut became a composting toilet, and a larger one was the wood-fired sauna. If no musicians played from the stage, it became an elevated relaxation area complete with a couch. Every piece of architecture and adornment carries Jim O's signature cleverness and handiwork. A master scrounger, Jim O' finds all manner of castoff wood and metal, which he turns into useful and beautiful furnishings and displays. He can build almost anything using his circular saw and screw gun.

In that original South Austin location, live oak trees stretched over the proceedings, and a bamboo forest crowded the lot's lower corner. Jim O' plants flowers and vegetables in any available space. Castor beans are an especial favorite because they grow fast and impart a prehistoric greenness to the scene. If rain has soaked the ground, he spreads a layer of straw. If rain continues, Jim O' erects a plethora of plastic roofs, and the show goes on.

All ages come to the gathering: graying hipsters, middle-aged cool folk and small children with their parents or grandparents. Kids play with one another and run around being kids.

Like at other such parties, there's always an early crowd, a middle group and some late arrivals. In the South Austin incarnation, a big influx of revelers arrived from Body Choir, an aerobic dance cadre who would meet earlier in the evening on Wednesdays. With new, refreshed folks came different edibles and heightened energies.

Anytime newcomers walk in, Jim O' introduces himself and implores them to "look around and see where you fit in." No matter the weather, every shirt he wears has had the sleeves ripped off, revealing his firm, bulging triceps. On his head sits a battered cowboy hat.

Early birds help set up, and late-stayers assist with breakdown and cleanup. It's not unusual for a few of the latter to spend the night, sleeping in tents, beneath tables or on a couch.

Austin's enormous popularity has created unintended and, for some, undesirable effects, such as gentrification. Areas close to the central city have gone up in value, which has increased taxes. It has become more expensive to own property, and landlords are forced to charge their tenants more or to sell. This was the scenario for Jim's increasingly desirable little hilltop corner lot. The owner decided in early 2008 to hand the Melridge place over to developers, who in turn planned to build condominiums. Jim O' had to vacate, so he began his search for a new site.

Plenty of stuff needed a new home, as well, and Jim sponsored a string of yard sales and giveaways while seeking his next hearth. Trucks and trailers full of junk made their way to the dump. Meanwhile, Jim O' strengthened his resolve to never again be a renter. Meanwhile, this generous individual found all sorts of assistance from the community of friends he'd nurtured for a score of years. Everyone involved was just as anxious as the man himself to resume the fellowship.

In mid-2008, O'Brien found what seemed to be an ideal new domicile: close to an acre of land on a bypassed side street off far South Congress. It is a narrow lot with a diminutive street frontage, but it widens toward the back, where flows Williamson Creek. Three or four derelict structures thereon presented themselves for fixing up. The area's zoning allows mobile structures, so one of the first to be moved on was a 1950s-vintage Spartan trailer. This and the nicest existing house were the first structures

Jim renovated, the former becoming his bedroom-bath-living space and the latter his office.

Within a few months, he'd moved on more portable buildings, trailers and campers and planted gardens. Jim O' received ample assistance from the community and a string of temporary tenant-helpers, who greatly eased the tasks of fixing up and settling in. Thanks also to his trademark indefatigability, soon sheds and barns arose around the lot from salvaged and repurposed lumber and galvanized roofing. The potlucks were rechristened "picnics," and to the patrons' delight, the monthly gatherings resumed.

Because of its location bordering a live creek, Jim's place features a goodly number of trees and vines next to the stream. He began selectively clearing that area and established a pleasant seating circle around a fire pit in sight of the rugged cliffs across the current. Here visitors could pitch tents and spend the night. Next came a nature trail through the remaining woods and a yard full of chickens and goats. Jim O' began to call the two acres his "Farmette."

The potlucks occur on the second Wednesday of each month, year round. In his catering business, known as Fine and Fancy Foods, Mr. O'Brien provides vegetarian selections such as stir-fry and other healthy options like gyros. He's a favorite provider at big Austin outdoor events, especially Eeyore's Birthday and Kerrville Folk Festival. His teams consist of numerous long-term friends and always several young people, many of whom are working their first jobs. Specialties include honey lemonade and the aforementioned chai.

What will you bring to the potluck?

26

MOONLIGHT BAT FLOAT

I t's nice to have something to count on every month.

The Texas River School (TRS) brings kids and rivers together. Led by Canadian Joe Kendall, the school's stated mission is to use nearby rivers as classrooms to teach and reinforce traditional academic subjects; to introduce important personal growth initiatives like leadership, self-discipline and civic responsibility; and to foster a lifelong connection to and affection for Texas waterways. TRS was formed with the intention of combining outdoor education, canoeing skills and swimming with healthy nutritional reinforcement. More than five thousand area youths are recipients of the services.[60]

In addition to working with students, the TRS hosts public events on Lady Bird Lake and Guadalupe River trips in conjunction with the Kerrville Folk Festival. Not only do the kids' groups learn about all things riparian, but they also enjoy listening to and singing along with such ecologically oriented musicians as Bill Oliver and members of his Otter Space Band. Adults and families can get in on the act during a monthly paddle.

Whereas, Snake Island occurs most often on the precise evening of the full moon, TRS offers a Moonlight Bat Float on the Saturday closest to the full moon. If you attend, you haul yourself down to the Texas Rowing Center on the lake's north shore just down from Austin High School. You walk out onto the floating dock and meet the other participants as well as Kendall's congenial staff. Since you reserved, your name is on the list, and you are assigned a canoe or kayak, either of which comes with paddles and a

Captain Bilgewater, aka Mr. Habitat and Bill Oliver, heads his Otter Space Band at a Texas River School benefit concert. *Author's collection.*

personal flotation device (PFD) for each passenger. You could either go solo or with a couple new friends.

As soon as all are assembled, Kendall delivers an orientation, telling you what to expect, demonstrating rudimentary technique and advising you on safety rules. Most accidents occur either getting into a boat or out of one, you learn, so you're careful as you climb into your craft and shove off. There could be upward of thirty other vessels joining the fun. If you're lucky, the *Lady of the Lake* raft is heading your way eastward, as well, supporting Bill Oliver and his silly and serious music. One of his backup singers is Linda Overton, wife to Joe Kendall and a director of TRS.

Depending on the time of year, you're likely to see many other folks out enjoying the water. Stand-up paddling has become quite popular, and you'll see some peddle-paddlers, as well. You get great views of Zilker Park and other shore features as you continue the two-mile voyage under bridges of Lamar Boulevard, Pflugerville Pedestrian and South First Street. At last, there's Congress and the remarkable Bat Bridge, officially named for Ann Richards. It's getting close to dusk, and you see a line of people along the east sidewalk on the bridge above you. They're also full of anticipation for the 1.5 million flying mammals that will soon emerge. On the lake at your level are several commercial and party boats, also full of watchers.

At dusk or just after, one or two "scouts" from the bat colony will test the air and light, darting out from the concrete crevices and back in again. Then, on a good night, as if responding to a central signal, the bats pour forth in two or three streams. Often, so many come out in such thick currents that they appear on weather radar. The Mexican Free-Tails head downstream, winging hundreds of miles and eating pounds of insects on their nightly excursions. People at this daily Austin party applaud.

It's almost dark now, so you follow the other canoes and kayaks back upstream to the dock, turn in your craft to the staff and head to your next celebration. By being part of this adventure, you've helped keep kids and rivers—not to mention yourself—healthy.

NOTES

1. Joseph Campbell, *The Power of Myth* (New York: Doubleday, 1988).
2. Diane Warner, *Big Book of Parties* (Franklin Lakes, NJ: Career Press, 1999).
3. "Topophilia," Wikipedia.org. Also mentioned in Joshua Long, *Weird City* (Austin: University of Texas Press, 2010).
4. Texas History 101, seventh grade.
5. Washington, D.C., and Brasilia, Brazil.
6. Joe Nick Patoski, from a quote overheard in a writers' workshop, January 2014.
7. "Decriminalization of Non-medical Cannabis in the United States," Wikipedia.org. In theory, Texas law enforcement officers have the option of ticketing offenders in possession of fewer than four ounces (a class B misdemeanor) instead of arresting. In practice, however, Travis County (Austin) is one of the few counties that opts for this (Harris County policy follows similar suit). Most such cases get dismissed in Travis County after the offender pays a fine, provides community service or takes drug classes, depending on such factors as the details surrounding the arrest and the offender's criminal history. In most places, e.g. College Station, officers will arrest offenders for any amount of marijuana whatsoever.
8. Speedway.
9. The mansion was originally built by Leonard Waller Groce, whose mother was cousin to Edwin Waller, Austin's designer and first mayor.
10. City of Austin website, http://austintexas.gov (accessed March 23, 2014).
11. Francis Edward Abernathy, ed., *Legendary Texas Ladies* (Denton: University of North Texas Press, 1994).
12. Connie Patterson, "Porter, William Sydney," *Handbook of Texas Online*, https://www.tshaonline.org/handbook/online/articles/fpo20 (accessed May 11, 2014).
13. The point can well be made that Austin's next great "salon" happened anytime naturalist Roy Bedechek, folklorist J. Frank Dobie and historian Walter Prescott Webb held dialogues at Barton Springs.
14. Lakes Buchanan, Inks, LBJ, Marble Falls, Travis, Austin and Lady Bird, although the last is operated by the City of Austin.
15. *Austin American-Statesman* archives, accessed August 26, 2014.

16. Aralyn Hughes, interview with the author, March 27, 2014.

17. Jacob Larmour, a prominent architect, designed many a Texas courthouse.

18. Aralyn Hughes, ed., *Kid Me Not* (Austin, TX: Violet Crown Publishers, 2014).

19. According to eyewitnesses, the Lid-O-Matic was a drawer in which sat several prepackaged ounces of marijuana and a cash box. If Palace residents weren't at home, you could leave your ten dollars in the box and choose a baggie. No one ever abused this system.

20. Mick Vann, "Oh, Oh, Those Summer Bites," *Austin Chronicle*, July 9, 1999, http://www.austinchronicle.com/food/1999-07-09/522329.

21. Kerry Awn, Artly Snuff and Theresa "Mrs. Snuff," interview with the author, June 5, 2014.

22. Jim Franklin, interview with the author, June 25, 2014.

23. SPAM is a registered trademark of the Hormel Corporation.

24. 709 Bee Cave Road.

25. David D. Arnsberger and John Booher, *Spamarama: The Cookbook* (Austin, TX: Whole Hog Productions, 1998).

26. I was that cop, by the way. I still own the hat.

27. Fletcher Clark, interview with the author, August 20, 2014.

28. It is Spanish for "balconies."

29. Michael McGeary, interview with the author, August 20, 2014.

30. Two, one on each side.

31. The Huns, *Live at the Palladium, 1979*, Get Hip Records reissue liner notes.

32. Joe Bryson, interview with the author, August 13, 2014.

33. Newman Stribling, longtime manager, quoted in the documentary *Viva Les Amis*, directed by Nancy Higgins.

34. Ray Oldenburg, *The Great Good Place*, 3rd ed. (New York: Marlowe & Company, 1999).

35. Hollywood-era murals on the side and a marquee out front.

36. Military- or band-style helmets.

37. From the Carnaval website.

38. Tuesdays.

39. Peter Mongillo, "Despite Growth, Old Settler's Music Festival Retains Its Intimacy," Austin360.com, http://www.austin360.com/news/entertainment/music/despite-growth-old-settlers-music-festival-retai-2/nRm5r (accessed May 7, 2014).

40. Salt Lick website, http://www.saltlickbbq.com/pages/FAQ.html (accessed April 19, 2014).

41. Thomas W. Cutrer, "McCulloch, Benjamin," *Handbook of Texas Online*, http://www.tshaonline.org/handbook/online/articles/fmc34 (accessed April 17, 2014). Benjamin McCulloch was an Indian fighter, Texas Ranger, United States marshal, surveyor, scout and brigadier general in the army of the Confederate States of America. His military career spanned the Texas Revolution and the Mexican War, and his hero's death in battle in 1862 ensured him a place in history. In 1896, a group of Confederate veterans founded a reunion ground here and named it in McCulloch's honor. Their annual meeting, usually around the full moon of June, attracted between five and six thousand old soldiers and their families. In 1936, beneath the live oaks around the Alamo-themed pavilion, several dozen stone and concrete picnic tables appeared, each with some Confederate individual or regiment engraved in the table top. The last old soldiers had passed on by 1947.

42. Dorman H. Winfrey, "Camp Ben McCulloch," *Handbook of Texas Online*, http://www.tshaonline.org/handbook/online/articles/voc01 (accessed April 17, 2014).

43. Camp Ben Reunion Official Site, http://www.campben.com/History.php (accessed April 17, 2014).

44. Reagan Brown, interview with the author, April 13, 2014.

45. Cody Johnson, interview with the author, May 4, 2014.

46. Grace Park, interview with the author, April 13, 2014.

47. "The last erection of an impotent administration," quoted in James L. Haley, *Passionate Nation* (New York: Free Press, 2006).

48. Austin Parks Foundation website, austinparks.org (accessed April, 8, 2014).

49. E.M. Pease was from Connecticut.

50. M.B. Lamar was a painter in oils and a poet. He designed an odd pair of baggy pants that were roomy enough for comfortable riding, the next big thing in equestrian fashion. The idea never caught on.

51. Austin Fire Museum in the Art Deco fire station, open only occasionally.

52. "O. Henry Pun-Off," Wikipedia.org (accessed May 11, 2014).

53. Delta Lady.

54. Fuller.

55. Oat Willie, whose campaign headquarters is a long-standing Austin headshop.

56. Copyright © 1991 Nels Jacobson. This article first appeared in Wes Wilson's poster journal *OFFtheWALL*.

57. Leeann Atherton, interview with the author, August 24, 2014.

58. James Talbot, interview with the author, August 25, 2014.

59. Jim O'Brien, interview with the author, April 9, 2014.

60. Texas River School website, https://texasriverschool.org/about (accessed May 13, 2014).

INDEX

ABOUT THE AUTHOR

Howie Richey is a curious fellow who has long been fascinated by the things people celebrate and how they do it. His formal background in Texas geography and audio production reveals little about his own capacity to jubilate, by either joining the closest party or by throwing one of his own. Nor do his forty-plus years as an Austin resident or his too-long career as a proofreader hint at the kind of company he keeps. He's a teacher, public speaker, radio personality, cartographer, woodworker, inveterate camper, blogger and community facilitator. Howie doesn't know everyone in Austin but is working on it. This is his first book.